LYING
DOG-FACED
PONY SOCIALISTS

*A Call to Save
Free Markets*

MADISON MOORE

Post Hill
PRESS

A POST HILL PRESS BOOK
ISBN: 978-1-64293-744-2
ISBN (eBook): 978-1-64293-745-9

Cover art by Cody Corcoran

Post Hill Press
New York • Nashville
posthillpress.com

Published in the United States of America
1 2 3 4 5 6 7 8 9 10

To my grandfather, James Earl Huntley Jr., who is supposed to lend me five dollars until payday.

And to my mom, Elizabeth Lee, who sacrificed every comfort in her life to provide every opportunity in mine...and who loved me even when I was a leftist.

CONTENTS

PREFACE:
FIFTEEN MINUTES
OF FAME

"I don't really care to see Joe Biden," I told my professor. "Can I stay at the hotel until y'all come back?"

"We're not here to reinforce your beliefs," he said. "We're here to get you to learn. You're going."

Fair enough.

I sluggishly dragged myself out of my shared hotel bed and dressed for the day.

"Don't try to dress to impress," my professor had explained before the trip. "We'll be knocking on doors and trying to stay warm. School clothes are fine."

He had me at "don't try." I had accordingly packed my comfortable quasi-hobo clothes, happily leaving my makeup in Georgia (mistake #1).

I wasn't opposed to hearing him speak, but we had already seen all the Democratic presidential candidates give their stump speeches at a massive event in Manchester, New Hampshire, the night before. I felt little desire to listen to Biden lecture aimlessly about job loss, cancer, and death. Nothing personal, I just had enough stress of my own with an eighteen-hour course load. I thought my time would be better spent sleeping in than listening to a litany of problems void of any concrete solutions.

I doubt my professor anticipated the massive impact that his answer would have on my life. I sure didn't.

With my early morning fate sealed, I accepted the event as an opportunity. After all, I planned to craft my final course paper on Joe Biden's primary performance in light of the impeachment trials. What better source for details than the candidate himself? Upon arriving at the venue, we sifted into the surprisingly short line, and the question hit me like a freight train: *How do you explain the performance in Iowa, and why should the voters believe that you can win the national election?* This was my chance to go directly to the source, and I wasn't about to waste it (you know, since I didn't exactly have a choice).

Vice President Biden concluded his stump speech and began fielding questions from the audience. After two or three questions, he called on me and handed me the mic. I'm generally a pretty confident person, perhaps too much, but in that moment it all evaporated. Even though I felt little interest in Biden personally, I couldn't help but be immensely intimidated by the Grand Canyon-sized power gap between us. This man had worked in close quarters on classified national security issues with President Obama, and I had dropped out of school last semester after failing all of my classes. To say I was nervous would be an understatement.

As respectfully as I knew how, I shot my question.

He shot back his own.

"Iowa's a democratic caucus. Have you ever been to a caucus?" he asked.

My nerves acted without my consent. Without thinking or hesitation, I nodded affirmatively, even though I had not been to a caucus (mistake #2).

"No, you haven't. You're a lying dog-faced pony soldier. You gotta be honest," Joe Biden quipped at me, and the audience laughed.

I felt my stomach drop and my heart accelerate. The former vice president of the United States just called me a liar on what was effectively national TV. How could I have been anything other than humiliated? He continued basking in the ease of softball questions for the next fifteen minutes or so, which helped redirect the room's attention and minimally assuage my embarrassment. He concluded the town hall and stuck around for handshakes, pictures, and even a cringe-worthy Backstreet Boys parody from my classmates...which went viral.

As the crowd began to disperse, I found myself suddenly swarmed by mics, cameras, and lights. Numb, I saw the grim reaper of the media before me, ready to hammer the last nail into the coffin of the liar. I had screwed up big-time, and I can honestly say I've never felt so terrified. I mustered a rambling answer in which I attempted to diffuse the conflict. Critiquing only his speech content and momentum, I had no intention of further picking any fights with the former vice president of the United States.

After the cameras lost interest in me, I mingled around the venue, making small talk and taking a couple more interviews as journalists from various media outlets approached me. Buzzfeed, the *Washington Post*, and others asked me what I thought about his response. I delivered as best I could honest answers, always noting I had not been to a caucus but simply got nervous in my response. My professor, my classmates, and I then loaded into the car, on our way to pick up some lunch.

We arrived at the restaurant and I called my parents, tears already flowing in a steady stream. The reality of the situation paralyzed me with fear: this was big news, I was at the center of it, and I had zero control of how it would be interpreted or perceived. I knew Joe Biden had sold me a nonreturnable, nonrefundable ticket to cancellation. I was done for. Rightly or wrongly, I had become the lying dog-faced pony soldier, and it was international news.

My email inbox steadily filled with new mail; most of it wasn't concerning my overdue library books. The media attention came in waves, as did my paralyzing helplessness to regulate what was shown or what was said. By the end of the week, my question and Biden's response to it had been covered by nearly every major and minor news outlet in America as well as a few in the UK and Australia. The video had been retweeted by Donald Trump Jr., mocked by Stephen Colbert and Trevor Noah, discussed by former speaker of the House Newt Gingrich and Ben Shapiro, and dissected by countless others. Most were critical of Biden and gracious toward me. I will never be able to fully express my gratitude for that favorable outcome.

As an extremely private person, I never wanted a stranger to search my name and find personal information about my life. For this reason, I didn't use public social media before this encounter, but I couldn't allow fear to keep me from speaking truthfully about my experience with Biden. Hiding became pointless. The same day he insulted me, an otherwise uneventful

February 9, he dropped an astonishing three points in the national polls. The following week, as the media covered my response and as he came in fifth in the New Hampshire primary (receiving zero delegates), he dropped an additional 5.2 points in the national polls. It was the most precipitous, continuous decline of any candidate in the 2020 presidential race at the time, and it was the only time Biden ceded his frontrunner position in the polls to Bernie Sanders. I went from anonymous to recognizable overnight—something I had neither requested nor anticipated.

More than this, I found it strange that his insult to me should be the one to go viral. Combative interactions with voters were hardly new for Joe Biden. Since starting his 2020 campaign for the presidency, he had already called other voters "fat," "liars," and told them to simply "vote for someone else." In fact, he had even used the same insult he used on me when talking to another college student during a different campaign. It didn't make any news waves then. What was so special about this interaction? And then I realized that the only voters he had accosted were men. Only men were asking him questions critical enough to elicit a confrontational response. I happened to be the first woman he verbally accosted on the campaign trail, and for whatever reason, people really took notice.

If all I contributed to the 2020 election cycle was to accidentally highlight Biden's bizarre rudeness to voters, I will consider my civic duty fulfilled. However, there is some lesson to be taken from the fact that the media took serious notice when he accosted a young woman but not when he accosted many men. I'm not sure precisely what, but there has to be something said for that.

Not the End: The Beginning

As difficult as it was to endure, this bizarre, unexpected notoriety lit an incessant flame inside of me. Before the Biden debacle, I, like many, had become resigned, if not satisfied, to settle for a life of anonymity. Apart from my intense desire to become the next Hannah Montana at eleven years old, I never wanted fame...but to be known for this would be infinitely worse than anonymity. Just imagine being remembered solely as the "lying dog-faced pony soldier." Who wants that for their life? For their mark on the world? Hard pass.

I knew I had to find a way to distinguish my life and my work from the seemingly inescapable brand Joe Biden had stamped on my forehead. I didn't know *when* or *how* or *why*. I simply knew deep in my gut this wasn't over. This book, in one sense, is not only an attempt to reclaim my identity from a well-known politician stamping me with an unforgettable insult, it is also an attempt to capitalize on this accidental notoriety for a productive purpose. I didn't ask for a platform, but I got it. When life gives you lemons, you take time to consider the economic systems that allowed for lemons to be both profitable and accessible on the consumer market.

Okay, maybe not all that, but...you get the point.

Coincidentally, I was undergoing somewhat of a political and philosophical metamorphosis at the time. I grew up in a culturally and politically conservative home and carried many of those same values into college: work hard, make your own way in life, give back, and remember God is watching (basically, don't be an idiot). Having spent the better part of two years immersed in perhaps the most concentrated leftist circles in America—the college debate community—I felt politically homeless.

For my first two years of college, I bought and practiced as best I knew how the leftist doctrines of wokeness, intersectionality, and admiration for socialism. I denounced my skin color, the supposed privilege that came with it, and my country that had ever only perpetuated injustice. As much as was needed to maintain my left-of-center identity, I spoke the lingo, took offense often, and disdained "whiteness" wherever I found it. Including my own skin.

Coming from a regular public high school, I entered college with zero understanding of the ideology I was being sucked into or of the pernicious origins and implications of such beliefs. Though I had phenomenal teachers, I was ill equipped for what lay ahead. Ever so subtly, I had been primed for this since middle school. Every Black History Month that rolled around, I was reminded of the evils that white men, my race, had inflicted on black people. While I believe our history is important to learn in its entirety, such framing of racial conflict fomented my internal hatred of white people and the country they had built.

But deep down, I secretly detested the identity politics and the woke intersectionality that I felt needlessly pitted various groups against each other. I played the part as best I could, not seeing any alternative. I only understood conservatives and capitalists as greed-driven parasites who would stop at nothing for a profit, destroying the environment in the process.

My bitter, leftist heart only began to thaw toward conservatism when I befriended a newbie debater on our team. His name was Christian Watson. He was black, libertarian, and as sharp as they come, and we spent countless late nights studying, arguing, and snacking in the library. Every time I would discuss any political topic, I would make some caveat for the plight of black people, overly careful about my consideration for their struggles should he misinterpret my analysis as racist.

Exasperated, he once told me, "Madison, you don't have to say this stuff all the time because I'm black. You don't have to worry about making these silly concessions. I'm not my skin color. I'm an individual. I'm Christian Watson, and I'm perfectly free."

That struck me.

Only then did I realize my ideology had me walking on eggshells anytime I was around a black person. I wanted to be extra careful, super considerate, always conceding for their massive struggle lest I slip up and commit the unforgivable sin of accidental racism. Christian opened my eyes to the reality that leftist intersectionality reduces people to their immutable characteristics and pits groups against each other. Still worse, it fosters an oppressor/oppressed dynamic that disallows individuals from interacting with/treating each other as equals.

We weren't a black man and a white woman interacting. We were Christian and Madison spending time together as friends. Though I can't explain quite how, our friendship solidified my secret belief that wokeness could never lead us to the post-racial harmony America desperately needed.

But I hadn't yet come full circle. After all, there was an election coming up.

Coming Full Circle

With the upcoming election, I felt conflicted about which candidate to throw my support behind. I had voted for Donald Trump in 2016 for two basic reasons. 1) I had done research on the tragedy in Benghazi and felt I could not in good conscience vote for former secretary of state Clinton, and 2) I felt that based on my values, Donald Trump was the more likely of the candidates to appoint a constitutionally minded judge to the vacancy on the Supreme Court. We could survive four years of Trump, but the SCOTUS appointment would affect U.S. legal proceedings for decades to come. Beyond that, I didn't care for Trump. I didn't like him much, but I felt he was the lesser of two evils, as many feel when they cast their vote for a candidate. The chaos and venom that surrounded this man felt so difficult to navigate, and I had bought many of the lies the media had proliferated about Trump. The hysteria that followed everything he did or said or tweeted felt impossible to navigate with accuracy.

Still feeling politically homeless, I went into the primaries unsure whom to throw my support behind. The candidate that appealed to me above all the rest was Andrew Yang. I had watched an hour-long interview of him and was awestruck by his charisma, heart, and intellect.

He was the only candidate in the Democratic Party who wasn't divisively harping about race and had very sensible reasoning for all of his policy proposals. I pursued him as a candidate further and liked most of what I found. He seemed to be the only candidate not actively vilifying Trump voters or condescending to us as racist, bigoted political inbreds. I liked him, and I still do. In fact, go watch the video of him suspending his campaign for the presidency in 2020. I am standing directly behind him on the verge of tears. I was Yang Gang full throttle, having even been thrown out of a Trump rally for wearing Yang gear (the primary in New Hampshire was undoubtedly the most eventful week of my life). However, my political transformation has brought me out of the Yang Gang I very much adored.

After I returned to Georgia, the election grew intensely personal for me. I followed every news story, poll, and report with an unhealthy, fervent obsession. Mainstream media outlets seemed to entirely ignore the very obvious reality that Biden was mentally unfit to fill the most powerful position in America and arguably the world. More than that, I was—stupidly—irritated to see the brazen disrespect with which he could treat a voter and carry on as if he were still the man of the people. He clearly felt superior to the commoners he descended to engage with, and it irked me to see him carry on seemingly unbothered and unconcerned about the average people he publicly humiliated on the way. He so transparently disdained the people he wanted to vote for him.

The very same semester I accidentally stumbled into viral fame, I was working my way through a class called Moral Foundations of Capitalism. It sounded like a paradox to me, but in an attempt to demonstrate my own "open-mindedness," I had enrolled. The class was absolutely transformative. Our extensive reading list encompassed the entire economic spectrum.

From Karl Marx and Friedrich Engels to Ayn Rand and Milton Friedman, the writers touched me firsthand without the discoloration of anyone else's interpretation. I am immensely grateful for the opportunities I had to take the class, to ask hard questions, and to freely engage in what I believe are some of the most important issues on the voting ballot. This book, in part, is my chance to extend that opportunity to others who may not have been so lucky in their academic or learning experience.

As I immersed myself in the academic and popular writings on these issues, I found a disconcerting trend. It seemed there was an important lesson to take home:

> *Free market enterprise allows for the massive innovation and progression we desperately need to meet the challenges of our times. It is the system that best taps into desperately needed innovation and progress.*

But this lesson was little known to college students like myself. Those who needed to hear the message most, millennials and Generation Z, were either not learning it or being pushed out of the conversation. The mainstream discussion on these topics, in my opinion, was heavily tainted by an unbearable condescension toward young people. The snowflakes, the Bernie Bros, the know-nothings were a problem to be solved, not a demographic to be reached.

Moreover, the field of economics unfortunately seemed to be somewhat of a boys' club. Do not misunderstand me: there is nothing wrong with boys' clubs (boys are great!), but there is a problem when women, who compose roughly half the American voter base, aren't a part of the conversation on the economy, one of the most critical voting issues on the ballot. In my time at the economics department at Mercer, I always felt honored to be invited to the exclusive colloquiums on economic issues with local business leaders, prominent authors, and accomplished professors. However, I couldn't help but notice every time I attended, I was the only woman at the table.

In my opinion, the most ardent example of this disappointing trend was Bob Lawson's *Socialism Sucks*. To be fair, I found his book full of convincing anecdotal evidence and excellent economic analysis. When I met Dr. Lawson, he was nothing but kind to me. However, I took issue not with his content but his *presentation*. The book was tainted, by his own admission, with "low-grade misogyny."

I don't consider myself politically correct, but I sure don't see the need for any degree of misogyny in economics or any other academic field for that matter. Again, his insight and analysis were adept. He is a brilliant man. But it was so much more difficult to accept when sprinkled with jokes of infidelity, degradation of women, and more. More importantly, his accessible economic analysis was the least geared for the demographic who needed to hear it the most. You won't change young people's minds by giving them solid ammunition to call you a sexist. If you really want to reach them, misogynistic jokes are not the way to do it. While I wouldn't pretend I'm Dr. Lawson's academic equal, my message is mostly the same as his: *socialism sucks*.

The goal of this book is to equip college students, and freethinkers more generally, with some of the basic information they need to navigate the competing economic systems increasingly present on the ballot, free of any "low-grade misogyny" or other unpleasantries. I may detest political correctness, but our standards for appropriate discourse should not disintegrate entirely in our fight to defend the marketplace of ideas.

Why Bother?

If you're a college student who cares about the future of America, this book is for you. If you're a skeptical voter unsure of how to navigate economic policies on the ballot, this book is for you. If you're simply a curious mind looking to bolster your argumentative ammo on capitalism and socialism, this book is for you.

In the following chapters, you will encounter what I hope is a detailed exploration of the competing economic policies in the American political landscape.

- The first chapter, "Sugary Sweet Socialism," explores the serious issues socialism is supposed to solve and the ways they make it seem just so sweet!
- The second chapter, "Socialism Unpacked," clears up some definitional fog, explores a little history, and looks at just how we keep coming back for more socialism.
- Chapter 3, "An Immortal Faith," discusses socialism's newest life support that somehow keeps us resuscitating ole Karl Marx.
- The fourth chapter, "Free Market Enterprise on Trial," discusses the concerns that free market enterprise is not

helping everyone it should and presents the reasons we
have to be encouraged by progress.

- The fifth chapter, "Free Market Enterprise: The Moral
  Choice," analyzes the foundational principles that make
  free market enterprise the moral choice, not just the
  effective one.
- Chapter 6, "The Legitimate Critiques of Free Market
  Enterprise," explores some of the biggest critiques of free
  market enterprise, and why these concerns are worth
  exploring.
- The seventh chapter, "Boris Yeltsin's Infatuation,"
  demonstrates not only the historical dominance of free
  markets as the primary force in improving human life,
  but also the little-known advances that have made it
  indispensable over the last two hundred years.
- In chapter 8, "Dog-Faced Pony Soldier, Over and Out!"
  I'll sum up my thoughts and share what I believe is at
  stake should we abandon our economic system of prosperity and plenty.

I want to make my motivations as transparent as possible.
Undoubtedly, the economy directs the most intimate and personal facets of our everyday lives. From infant mortality to life
expectancy, the health of the economy determines a vast array
of critical issues, many of which are a literal matter of life and
death. It determines the ability of the average American to put
food on the table, keep a roof over their head, and to whatever
extent possible, pursue happiness.

Most importantly, I want to challenge the notion that socialism is the moral answer for how we achieve this. College professors mostly tell us that free market enterprise is exploiting the working class, that socialism would bring us better results. They fail to mention that poor people enjoy a better standard of living in economically free societies. They fail to mention that poor people secure a greater *percentage* of overall wealth in these societies. They fail to inform us that free markets have ushered in the greatest period of human development and prosperity in the history of the world, called the Great Enrichment by some economic historians.

Simply put, we're not being told the whole story. If we actually care about the poor, we should seek to preserve and improve the system that has made their prosperity possible in the first place.

This book shouldn't be taken as an all-encompassing, exclusive assessment of economic policy. There are many valid, topical issues I simply don't have room to cover here. But such omissions should not be interpreted as deliberate, intentional, or deceptive. Rather, this book will touch on some of the most pressing issues I have seen regularly pop up in popular political and economic conversations.

I was granted a platform, and I am using it the best way I know how. The entirety of this book is my work and my voice guided by the simple but eternal words of Ralph Waldo Emerson: "Speak what you think now in hard words, and tomorrow speak what tomorrow thinks in hard words, though it contradict everything you said today."

CHAPTER 1

SUGARY SWEET SOCIALISM

The Panic

SEVERAL YEARS AGO, MY MOM, my three brothers, and I picked up a cheap fast-food dinner on our way home from a family outing. Packed in our minivan, we quickly passed around the hot food. Now, to be clear, the whole family loves food maybe a little too much, but it just so happened that this evening my youngest brother scarfed his down way too fast. Suddenly, in the midst of our gluttonous glee, we were interrupted by his shrill screaming.

"I can't breathe, I can't breathe!" my brother shrieked, clearly demonstrating that he could. In his haste, he had quite literally bitten off more than he could chew, resulting in an elongated, mostly intact mozzarella stick lodged down his throat. In the small confines of our aging minivan, he continued to scream, "Take me to the hospital—now!"

We attempted to help, trying to dislodge the ill-fated mozzarella stick. Between our belly-shaking laughter at the absurdity of the situation, alarmed concern for him, and aggravation at his high-pitched screaming in such close quarters, the brief problem returned us to our normal state of affairs: chaotic. Eventually, he successfully dislodged the cheese stick of doom, and we continued the trip back home, not to the hospital.

As funny as it was in the absurdity of the moment, my little brother felt desperate, scared, and panicked. He acted in accordance with his feeling of desperation by screaming and demanding to be rushed to the hospital. I recently recalled the incident from many years ago. We've laughed about the debacle many times since then. When I asked him if he felt, as the rest of us did, that he had overreacted, he simply responded, "No, I didn't."

These days it feels like many Americans, especially young Americans, are in a similar state of cheese-stick-stuck-in-the-throat panic. This desperation has led to the emergence of solutions and figureheads that were previously unthinkable in the realm of conventional American politics. But make no mistake: the calls for worrisome and risky political measures on both the left and the right are fueled by a fear-driven populism that we'll lose the future if we don't act now.

The reality of a scared public isn't hard to understand. From the sheer enormity of student debt to the doomsday predictions on climate change to the hollowing out of manufacturing and labor jobs in Middle America, we have no shortage of serious problems. In response to these challenges and others like them, nationalist populist movements have gained momentum both in America and around the world. Between a growing distrust in conventional institutions, such as the media, and a growing sense that things will not be as good for them as they were for previous generations, there are ample reasons to succumb to such serious desperation.

The 2008 Great Recession merely foreshadowed the problems we would face in the following decade. Countless college students are burdened with massive debt. They pose the next big economic bubble waiting to break us. At a staggering $1.5 trillion, student loans represent on average over $30,000 in debt for each of the forty-four million-plus students who shoulder this impending economic disaster. Is it any wonder we have candidates running on platforms of student debt cancellation?

Alternative options are equally unappealing. Prospects for those without a college degree grow ever more precarious. Not only has this segment of the workforce seen a disturbing, dramatic spike in deaths of despair—overdose, alcohol poisoning, and suicide—their prospects for the future are hardly sunny. Globalization, automation, and wage stagnation paint a grim future for the blue-collar American worker. In fact, one Democratic presidential candidate even attributed such job losses in manufacturing to Trump's 2016 victory.

Things have gotten so bad with the decimation of manufacturing jobs in Michigan, Ohio, Pennsylvania, Wisconsin, which were the swing states he [Trump] needed to win, we automated

away four million jobs in those states…look at the voter district data, there's a direct correlation with the number of industrial robots in the district and the movement toward Trump.
—Andrew Yang, in a 2019 interview
with *Simulation*

Who could blame young people for wanting better? You can't sell the American dream as the acceptance of tens of thousands of dollars of debt before even entering the job market, nor can you peddle it as a gamble for the bare minimum with the shrinking low-wage labor market.

Beyond this, concern for the environment now plagues our minds. We're already witnessing the effects of climate change. *National Geographic* says the average global temperature rose by an estimated 1.2 to 1.4 degrees over the last century, and 2019 concluded *the warmest decade on record* as confirmed by NASA, NOAA, and the U.K. Meteorological Office. We're watching ocean levels rise, and as a native coastal Floridian, that scares the pony soldier out of me. Many of our most prominent leaders left of center are ringing the alarm bells of the coming disaster of climate change while others on the right claim it doesn't exist at all: the cherry on top of our calamity concoction.

More than this, we feel…lost. Long before COVID-19, Americans were already struggling with a different type of epidemic: loneliness. According to the U.S. Health Resources and Services Administration, "Two in five Americans report that sometimes or always their social relationships are not meaningful, and one in five say they feel lonely or socially isolated." The government calls for "social distancing" could hardly come at a worse time. Our mental health is suffering too. Rates of "major depressive episode" among young people aged eighteen to twenty-five increased by 63 percent from 2009 to 2017, according to a study from the American Psychological Association. Suicide-related outcomes—including suicidal ideation, plans, attempts, and deaths by suicide—within the last year also increased over roughly the same period.

We're up against some serious problems. Our panic, fear, and desperation are not the fulfillment of the 'entitled millennial' trope or the dramatic panic of a seven-year-old with a cheese stick stuck in his throat. My generation faces its own, new giants, we haven't even touched on our broken health care system, exponential increases in income inequality, and the dangerously polarized political climate in which we find ourselves.

So How Can We Fix It?

According to the left, the answer is socialism. Democratic socialism to be exact. How exactly is democratic socialism distinguished from our

> If you're struggling with depression or thoughts of suicide, please call the National Suicide Prevention Hotline for help at 1-800-273-8255 or text BRAVE to 741741. Please consider reading Stephen Ilardi's The Depression Cure. This book pulled me out of the darkest, most painful period of my life. I hope it can help you too. Remember, you are loved, valuable, and needed. Life can get better, but death can never be undone.

current, mostly capitalist system? Let's take it straight from self-identified democratic socialist congresswoman Alexandria Ocasio-Cortez.

> *When we talk about ideas like, for example, democratic socialism, it means putting democracy and society first, instead of capital first. It doesn't mean that you put other things last; it doesn't mean that the actual concept of capital as a society should be abolished...but it's a question of our priorities.*

Credit where credit is due. AOC went from bartender to Congress all before she was thirty years old. She is arguably the most powerful Democrat on the Hill, if you're going on fundraising capabilities, but her definition of democratic socialism is...lacking.

AOC plays fast and loose with the term "capital" here, and the same applies to her frequent use of "capitalism." Her misunderstanding of the terms and the widespread nature of this misunderstanding are why I prefer the term "free market enterprise" as opposed to the term "capitalism."

Why? Well, as economic historian professor Deirdre McCloskey said in a recent interview, emphasis on the accumulation of capital does a disservice to the system of free enterprise—a system that fosters massive, widespread *innovation*. More than this, the term has taken on negative and derogatory connotations in recent years. By using "free market enterprise" instead, I'm doing my best to take Friedrich Hayek's advice on the matter: "If old truths are to retain their hold on men's minds, they must be restated in the language and concepts of successive generations."

But forgive me, I digress. Back to the question of democratic socialism. If you have trouble pinning down the definition you're not alone. Even Bernie Sanders sidesteps the question when asked directly.

> *What democratic socialism is about is saying that it is immoral and wrong that the top tenth of 1 percent in this country...own almost as much wealth as the bottom 90 percent. That it is wrong today, in a rigged economy, that 57 percent of all new income is going to the top 1 percent. That when you look around the world, you see every other major country providing health care to all people as a right except the United States. You see every other major country saying to moms that when you have a baby, we're not going to separate you from your newborn baby because we are going to have medical and family paid leave like every other country on earth.*

Wait, what? Let's break down Bernie Sanders's two basic appeals.

- First, it's a blatant attack against perceived unfairness and a full-on invocation of your potential envy. A few select people have so much, and you're only getting so little! How can that be? You should probably be angry about it! This should concern us. Any political appeal to our darkest natures of vengeance and envy never lead to anything good. We'll explore some of those historical examples later.

- Second, he presents a litany of eminently desirable outcomes to any reasonable person: free health care, paid maternity leave, higher wages, student debt cancellation, and free candy raining from the sky. Frankly, it all sounds fantastic. Seriously? Who would say no to that? Bernie Sanders is the Willy Wonka of government giveaways, and a vote for him is a golden ticket to the mystical factory of free government benefits. How could we ever vote otherwise?

I'd like to highlight what he does *not* say.

What we don't get here is a logical, ethical explanation for *how* we achieve these things. It sounds humanitarian, even philosophical, to say something is a human right, but it's much harder to actually make it happen in a way that doesn't violate other rights and just generally screw things up. Just ask the U.N...or Venezuela for that matter. Venezuela's popular conceptions of what constituted a human right only expanded before their nightmare, but a basic Google search on human rights in Venezuela will reveal only abuses. Venezuela's president, Nicolás Maduro, rose to power promising greater social spending on "housing, education, and health care." That should ring a few bells. Although various prosperous nations have nationalized health care, these systems also often pose significant problems like dangerously long waits and little to no avenues to ensure quality.

Now, to be fair to Bernie, this quote was taken from one of the televised debates in which candidates, by the very nature of the platform, are forced to repeat loud and proud their rehearsed talking points in a manner that resonates with the audience eating Pringles in their living rooms. It has to be simple. It has to be sweet. Democrats, Republicans, and independents alike follow this format, at least during much of the campaign season.

The problem is that democratic socialists like Bernie Sanders use this to their advantage and remain deliberately vague about what they want to do. While yes, this is only one quote from a debate, I read his book. More often than not, he presents much of the same. He rants about unfairness, tantalizes us with free benefits, and continues pulling at our heartstrings. He details his various relationships, experiences, and events. There isn't much in the way of policy. Why?

Democratic socialists are not stupid. They know that the means to achieve what they want are inherently undesirable to the general American public: more taxation with bigger, more powerful government, leaving less economic and social freedom for you. They deliberately employ a pathos-based appeal at nearly every step of the way because they don't want you thinking about who will be forced to pay their fifteen-dollar minimum wage; they want you thinking how nice it would be to have a "living wage." They don't want you thinking about the insanity of the government controlling *your* health care. They want you thinking about how every American deserves health care as a human right. They don't want you thinking about the mechanical factors that lead to some individuals producing more and consequently earning more. They want you enraged at the fact that some individuals are mega-wealthy, but you are not. It's all very predictable.

> *This is the key truth I uncovered, even before my silly run-in with Joe Biden: Socialism on the political level will only ever appeal to emotion, not to data or reason. Socialism is an appeal to the heart, not the head. While your heart might be perfectly useful for making you lovesick, it isn't exactly adept at navigating which economic policies on the ballot are prudent, effective, and just.*

Caring a great deal about an issue does not equate to having the best discernment on that issue. Feeling strongly is just not enough. We need to know what really works best for an economy.

Moreover, caring about issues like the scarcity of health care, radical income inequality, and maternity leave should prompt us to explore all possible solutions and weigh them on their merits and track record of producing the desired result. If you want to help a cause, whatever that cause may be, throwing your support behind the candidate who insists they care the most about that cause may not always get you what you want. Just because a politician says they care about an issue does *not* mean their policies are the best for solving it, and it is precisely when they loudly harp on their compassion and care that we ought to distrust them the most.

Politicians Know Best

What a wonderful country we have! The best-known socialist in the country happens to be a millionaire with three houses. What'd I miss here?

—Mike Bloomberg,
former New York City mayor

Socialist policies grow in lockstep with higher taxes. That's just the way it is. And if you oppose higher taxes, democratic socialist doctrine says maybe you just don't know what's best. Democratic socialists are, perhaps, more noble than you, more generous. They know how your money is best spent.

Allow me to demonstrate the superiority of the democratic socialist's ability to spend your money. I think you'll agree they're far more capable.

Socialism, after all, is government control of the means of production. Let me say that again: it is not generous liberalism or compassionate egalitarianism; it is government control of the resources we all need to survive and thrive. In order to procure greater control over such resources, a critical component of socialist thinking is high taxation to better enable the government to control and reallocate resources such as money. Exorbitant taxation is to socialism what peanut butter is to jelly.

Congresswoman Alexandria Ocasio-Cortez felt no hesitation in voting to give herself a raise on her already generous annual salary of $174,000 before having even completed an entire year in her elected position. Her reasoning? "Voting against cost-of-living increases for members of Congress may sound nice, but doing so only increases pressure on them to keep dark money loopholes open."

Remember, if you don't give Congress a raise on their salary, which is already over three times higher than the national average salary, you're incentivizing corruption. Shame on you. Don't you understand how your tax dollars are best spent?

All of this is apart from the fact that AOC lives in a luxury apartment that offers "access to private massage rooms, state-of-the-art hydrotherapy beds, saunas, a 25-meter indoor lap pool, a full-scale kitchen with wood-fired pizza oven, a rooftop pool with view of the Capitol, a fireside lounge featuring a Steinway & Sons player piano, a Peloton cycling studio, and a PGA-grade golf simulation lounge that allows users to play virtually on the world's most exclusive golf courses." Just the standard accommodations of working-class people, right? Remember, they know better.

Rest assured: from AOC's perspective, her housing just provides her with basic necessities such as "clean air" and "clean water." In fact, an affordable housing unit for senior citizens she toured apparently looked "just like hers." All on top of the fact that she went to one of the most expensive private universities in the country.

And Bernie Sanders? As he has ascended into the millionaire class following his sky-high book sales (which I have damningly contributed to), he has enjoyed more of that money, thanks to the tax cuts he received under President Trump. One might rightfully ask if perhaps he has redirected much of that money to charity instead of to the government. After all, the working people he supports are suffering greatly. Perhaps he views charity as a more effective means of change than government?

Nope. That would be wrong, but you shouldn't question it.

Sanders not only enjoys a relatively low income tax rate, thanks to Trump's cuts, he also gives very little to charity—only 3 percent of his income in his best year. More than this, he owns three houses, including an extravagant vacation home on Lake Champlain that he purchased for over half a million dollars.

Stay calm, though. He's ready to take down the bourgeoisie regardless of whether he became a member of it along the way.

And last but not least, congresswoman Ilhan Omar's campaign funneled a meager $800,000 to the consulting firm of the man with whom she was alleged to have had an affair. He is now her husband. Gee, sure hope those weren't grassroots-raised dollars!

What's the point I'm making with all of this? The point is that these politicians are neglecting to put their money where their mouths are. They want higher taxes for everyone else but are themselves milking the system behind the scenes. It's the redistribution of *your* wealth, not theirs. Stop complaining.

More importantly, these politicians suffer from what I would characterize as somewhat of a savior complex. They see these issues the American people face and feel it is their responsibility, their duty, to solve the problem. This is not to say that government intervention is never needed to fix a problem, but it should not be hailed as the central component of the average American's ability to live a decent and prosperous life.

What do I mean by this? We better ourselves through education. Who controls that education? The government. We maintain our health through our lifestyle and utilization of health care services. Who wants to take over our health care? The government. The list goes on and on. Some government is, of course, needed. We like roads, after all. But government control should not be the defining characteristic or provision of a good life, and increasingly, it's being hailed as the *only* path to that good life.

These politicians got rich with unapologetic capitalism. Free market enterprise. They've traded their services and talents for money. Whether I like it or not, Americans have purchased their services by electing them to positions of power and paying for their leadership.

But is that what they want for you? Do they think capitalism, free market enterprise, should play a role in your life? No, your path to prosperity is paved by them, the enlightened few, the democratic socialists. Sanders made clear his feelings about capitalism in his exchange with Anderson Cooper.

> *Cooper:* You don't consider yourself a capitalist though?

> *Sanders:* Do I consider myself part of the casino capitalist process by which so few have so much and so many have so little? By which Wall Street's greed and recklessness wrecked this economy? No, I don't. I believe in a society where all people do well, not just a handful of billionaires.

Cool. If you're really not a capitalist, then refund my book purchases, Senator Sanders. This is not rhetorical. If they really don't believe in this system, maybe they shouldn't have gotten rich off of it before openly vilifying it.

We shouldn't trust people who advocate paths to prosperity that look nothing like their own. AOC didn't get rich from welfare checks, and Bernie didn't make millions by roughing it in government housing. But you can be confident that you'll be slammed in the public political sphere if you *dare* say so.

Those Who Disagree Will Be Dealt With. Harshly.

Despite all this, Americans find themselves force-fed the crappy carrot mush of socialism. Democratic socialists constantly remind us that capitalists are the greedy, selfish hobgoblins who seek to improve nothing but the linings of their own wallets. Anyone who does not favor wealth redistribution, socialist programs, and greater government control does not care about the poor, they tell us. Those who oppose the rising wave of socialism best watch out lest it come crashing down on their heads like they're surfers with bad timing.

It's so outlandish I won't be surprised if I'm disbelieved, but after I signed the contract to write this book, I reached out to the most intelligent leftist professor I knew on campus. I didn't want to strawman the opposition, and hey, I'm new to this after all. I asked for his help. He told me he would *definitely not* help me. He told me that he thought my project was, and I quote, "terrible and evil." My own professor and extracurricular sponsor who had written me letters of recommendation did not hesitate to impugn my character for having the wrong opinion on economics.

But that's only the beginning.

Far worse than the militant insistence on socialism is the vitriolic character maligning one will face in open support of free market enterprise. You may say I'm overreacting, but if you've spent any significant amount of time on a college campus, chances are you've seen it too.

Underneath all the rhetoric, democratic socialists are telling you that socialism is merely a more generous form of *liberalism*. To be a real liberal is to support socialism, and if you don't, you're a bad person. "Put your money where your mouth is" seems to be the unspoken implication of the charge, regardless of the fact that it's others' money they're talking about.

After all, they say, socialism helps the poor, the disenfranchised, the marginalized. In the current American leftist perspective, these populations will equate to some rough combination of black people, minorities, LGBTQ+, and women, no matter how condescending that mindset may be toward those groups. The writers at the Foundation for Economic Education captured this sentiment perfectly in a recent article: "Just as Marxism demonized capitalists, critical race theory vilifies white people. Both try to foment resentment, envy, and a victimhood complex among the oppressed class it claims to champion."[1]

The current strand of democratic socialism seems to be a virulent fusion of the two: critical race theory and Marxist principles. We'll take a deeper dive into that later.

Regardless, I have seen time and again the swift arm of social justice fall hard and fast on the unsuspecting few who would even dare to politically define themselves as "socially liberal but fiscally conservative."

For instance, I recall an after-party in a hotel room with college students from all across the country. We had gathered in Boston on Harvard's dime to attend the university's National Campaign Conference. If you can imagine twenty college students crammed into a single hotel room downing shots and standing on tables to demand the room vote on the efficacy of consumer demands versus voting trends in producing legislative policy, that was precisely what happened that night. Thanks, Harvard. Your money was well spent.

Anyhoo, I remember before things got rowdy that night, we were sitting around having a civil political discussion when I made the grave mistake of describing myself as the irredeemable "socially liberal but fiscally conservative." A dark-haired girl with a sharp mind and an attractive face swiftly retorted, "So you want to pretend like you care about people, but you don't support legislation to actually help them?"

Caught off guard by her aggressiveness, I gave some half-hearted explanation of how I thought Walmart's production of cheap goods was a net positive for the everyday consumer. (Friendly heads up: if you're in a room full of liberals, or even decently educated individuals for that matter, do not try to formulate your position by defending Walmart as a great moral actor. You can thank me later.) After a hearty barrage on the horrors of child labor and sweat shops, I wimpily let the discussion die without putting up much of a fight (I was still in my quasi-lefty mentality at the time). I still couldn't articulate the value of free markets at the time or answer for legitimate critiques.

While this was merely embarrassing, the hostile public sphere is getting almost…scary. You may not recall this headline—after all, who cares about anything before the full-speed, nonstop crapfest of 2020?—but in June 2019, Governor John Hickenlooper received major flack for his comments during a democratic convention. He was running a strong campaign, and his chances of victory were roughly as good as my own prospects of getting selected in the first round of the NFL Draft. How did he step out of line?

He said, "If we want to beat Donald Trump and achieve big progressive goals, socialism is not the answer…" The audience answered his seemingly commonsensical political strategy with *vehement booing*, which only roared louder as he shot back, "You know, if we're not careful, we're going to end up reelecting the worst president in American history."

More than this, during the early portion of the 2020 primary cycle, we saw AOC, considered by many to be the "new face of the Democratic Party," refuse for a time to continue to support Bernie Sanders because he publicly touted his Joe Rogan endorsement. Rogan, a political liberal on a majority of issues, did not share AOC's perspectives on puberty-delaying hormones for trans children or the participation of biological males in women's sports. This was a deal-breaker. For those who may feel displays of political and cultural puritanism such as these push the extremes, she offered an unapologetic response, "For anyone who accuses us of instituting purity tests, it's called having values, it's called giving a damn." Do not resist our policies on the economy. Or on the culture. Those who do will be dealt with. Harshly.

These peripheral tidbits of forgotten political noise highlight two unsettling shifts. First, socialist puritanism is not confined to aging and irrelevant tweets. Ad hominem (character) attacks are routinely employed to silence political thought which strays from the leftist, socialist canon. If you step out of line, you are not simply in disagreement with the party, you are inherently immoral. I'm not saying this never happens on the right, but it's certainly getting much, *much* louder on the left. Second, the already minimal set of agreed-upon truths common to conservatives and liberals is shrinking by alarming margins. We are losing common ground. This should cause folks on all sides a reasonable degree of concern considering that unless we would like a full-out civil war, we have to get along on some basic level. It's harder to do that when we agree on so little. For decades, free market enterprise had been the sacred cow of American politics. Today it is the greed-fueled scourge of the American left. What happened?

The Perception of "Socialism" among the Young

In order to understand the dramatic shift of the left, we must also understand the fundamental differences in perceptions of socialism with each generation. The Baby Boomers, Gen Xers, and other older generations associate socialism with Cuba and the former U.S.S.R. Having lived through the Cold War, or having parents who did, the untouchable, inherently evil, thoroughly abhorrent nature of socialism was nonnegotiable for many. We had won World War II and the Cold War. History was over. Democratic capitalism had won once and for all, and the age of the Washington Consensus was thus ushered in. The very idea of resurrecting socialism, which had been intentionally hacked, sacked, and chucked, was and is ludicrous to them. Understandable.

But younger generations have had a very different experience. Remember, we're still in panic mode. Many young people, rightly or wrongly, associate many of these perils with our prevailing economic system: capitalism. As wealth continues to concentrate in the upper echelons of society in increasingly dramatic numbers, young people are desperate to pull the emergency plug on capitalism in hopes of something better.

But we're not looking to Russia or Cuba or Venezuela for our solutions. We're looking to the Nordic countries for our path forward: Sweden, Finland, Norway, the Netherlands. These are the countries that come to mind when young folks express their desire for a more socialist government, and who could blame them?

The Nordic countries, by almost any measure of success, are doing phenomenally well. From their life expectancy and infant mortality rates to their gender equality and technological development rankings, these countries rise to the top in terms of overall desirability. These small but industrious countries enjoy exceptional economic growth in combination with an expansive social safety net which provides a plethora of government services: elder care for all, universal health care, free public college for all, and more. So heck, why not give it a go here in the USA?

After all, the position that the U.S. health care system is fundamentally broken is one of the few perspectives almost all of us can agree on. Millennials and Gen Z want something better than what they've gotten, and they're not wrong for that. But they've incorrectly identified capitalism as the source of their woes and, consequently, are trying to solve it with the wrong solutions.

Most young folks fail to recognize the underlying realities that allow for such unparalleled prosperity in the Nordic countries. In most regards, these are capitalist economies. From strong private property laws to few business regulations, several Nordic countries, including Sweden and Denmark, rank above the United States in the Index of Economic Freedom, which scales countries according to how economically free (capitalist) they are. The success of the Nordic countries is not only fueled by intensely capitalist economies, it is further bolstered by other complex factors which largely contribute to its success. Apart from the fact that these countries administer intensely strict and highly selective immigration policies, they also pass on much of their military expenditures to the United States. Moreover, their highly homogeneous society enjoys high levels of social trust, civic engagement, and a robust culture that emphasizes hard work and cooperation. The success of the Nordic countries is the result of a complex set of cultural and demographic conditions as well as economic policies. It is not the self-evident utopian poster child of socialism. We'll go deeper into this later.

Millennials and Gen Z, including me at one time, have been wrongfully duped into thinking that the socialist utopia of the Nordic countries could easily be implemented here in the United

States if only we could overcome our own selfishness and greed. If only we could abandon dirty capitalism, we could fix all these problems. But we are not a homogeneous country. We boast hundreds of different cultural groups and ethnic backgrounds. And we don't have as strict immigration policies. We have generous stances, allowing hundreds of thousands of immigrants to join our country every year. To put it simply, we are not the Nordic countries. There's nothing wrong with that. Although they do boast impressive stats on a wide array of well-being measures, they have neither our diversity nor our inclusive approach to immigration. Both are worth preserving, and you cannot do that when you allow a welfare state to balloon. In the same way a lifeboat can hold only so many people, a tax base can support only so many free benefits.

> *Socialism is being pushed on young people extremely aggressively. After all, we are desperate for change to address the hysteria-inducing problems. But the solution to our woes is not to abandon free market enterprise.*

The deceptive allure of a more egalitarian society has been hijacked by political opportunists who seek to permanently alter America. We have to get smarter. We must equip ourselves with the right information to push back on this political and cultural beast. Thankfully, legislative changes in our representative republic tend to move slowly. We probably have time, but we have serious cause to be skeptical about this rising tide of socialist pride.

CHAPTER 2

SOCIALISM UNPACKED

We will take America without firing a single shot. We do not have to invade the U.S.; we will destroy you from within.
— Nikita Khrushchev, Premier of the U.S.S.R, November 18, 1956

Then Mary took about a pint of pure nard, an expensive perfume; she poured it on Jesus' feet and wiped his feet with her hair. And the house was filled with the fragrance of the perfume. But one of his disciples, Judas Iscariot, who was later to betray him, objected, "Why wasn't this perfume sold and the money given to the poor? It was worth a year's wages." He did not say this because he cared about the poor but because he was a thief;

as keeper of the money bag, he used to help himself
to what was put into it.
—John 12:3–6 New International Version

I F JUDAS ISCARIOT, THE ARCHETYPAL villain of Western society, were to run for political office in America today, I bet he'd run as a socialist. His feigned concern for the poor served only the purpose of increasing the funds from which he could steal for himself. He never cared about them. He was offended by Mary's generous display of affection for Jesus not because he took offense on behalf of the poor, but rather because he took offense on behalf of himself.

I worry we're falling for the same nasty trick. Concern for the poor from political leaders should always be met with immediate skepticism when their means to helping the poor does not involve the use of their own money but the forcible use of yours.

But socialism is the wet noodle of political terminology: impossible to pin down. The right often equates it with communism. The left often equates it with economic egalitarianism. Who is right? And what the heck is socialism? In order to understand the confusion behind this term, let's rewind for a moment to trace its origins.

What the Heck Is Socialism?

Socialism has somehow come to mean everything and nothing all at once, but looking back, it's easy to understand why. Unlike most other descriptive societal terminology such as "capitalism," "feudalism," or "liberalism," socialism emerged *before* it ever existed. In other words, these terms came into existence *with* or *shortly after* the creation of the systems they described. Socialism started as the description of an idea. It was a suggestion of *how* a society should be organized, not the description of how a given society already existed. Martin Malia, a Harvard-educated professor at UC Berkeley, described this phenomenon in his book *Soviet Tragedy: A History of Socialism in Russia*.

Thus, it makes sense that the term might be subject to controversy. Originally, it denoted an abstract idea. Even Karl Marx himself, known with Friedrich Engels as a father of socialism, made this distinction clear: "I arrived at the point of seeing the idea in reality itself."

Therefore, it is not initially self-evident. For example, if I say the term "apple," you immediately see in your mind's eye a ripe, firm fruit. It may be green, red, or even yellow, but the essential conception and picture of the term is immediately clear because it describes a concrete reality. The more abstract the concept, the more subjective and controversial its definition. This was and is the case with socialism. Malia notes the international history of this ongoing definitional conflict.

> *The term [socialism] has been plausibly claimed by Stalinist Russia, China of the Cultural Revolution, Sweden of the social democratic "middleway," Labourite Britain, Israel of the Kibbutzim, the cooperative community of Brook Farm, and the Khmer Rouge...[these socialisms] usually challenged the legitimacy of the others, and indeed have often anathematized [condemned] their rivals in shrill sectarian tones.*

You may have experienced this conflict yourself in political conversations. As we've already discussed, young people think the Nordic countries have socialism. Older folks think Venezuela and Cuba have socialism. The conversation evolves along predictable partisan lines also. Right-wingers emphasize the worst cases, and left-wingers emphasize the best cases. All in line with our infallible objectivity.

To avoid making such a mistake in this book, I will define only two kinds of socialism. First, we will look at the original idea and its basic prescriptions for society as laid out by the man most widely credited with its creation, Karl Marx. Second, we will look at the form of wildly popular socialism currently rising in America: democratic socialism. From there, we'll see how they relate and why they matter to America today.

Karl Marx, the OG Socialist

Though the term "socialism" did not originate with them, Karl Marx and Friedrich Engels were the first to give it a fully fleshed-out doctrine, which they laid out in their coauthored book *The Communist Manifesto*. Although Marx critiqued certain variations of socialism, he largely used socialism interchangeably with communism, and rather than muddy his words, I'll give them to you directly: "…the theory of communism can be summed up in a single sentence: Abolition of private property." Not quite a full sentence there, Karl, but we get the idea. It was likewise surmised in the now infamous mantra, "From each according to his ability, to each according to his needs." Marx defined socialism as part of a detailed prophecy of sorts for the future.

A socialist society was roughly defined by three primary characteristics:

- a simplified understanding of history as a conflict between the proletariat (working class) and the bourgeoisie (wealthy upper class);
- a collective approach to understanding humanity;
- government-controlled production and distribution of natural resources, the "means of production."

Such a society might be difficult to envision, but some of his desired outcomes already exist in the U.S.A. Marx gives ten markers of an ideal socialist/communist state. This helps highlight the ways in which we already embrace socialism as well as the logical extensions of the ideology.

1) the abolition of property in lands and application of all rents of land to public purposes;
2) a heavy progressive or graduated income tax;
3) abolition of all right of inheritance;
4) confiscation of the property of all emigrants and rebels;
5) centralization of credit into the hands of the State, by means of a national bank with State capital and an exclusive monopoly;
6) centralization of the means of communication and transport in the hands of the State;
7) extension of factories and instruments of production owned by the State, the bringing into the cultivation of waste lands, and the improvement of the soil generally in accordance with a common plan;

8) equal liability of all to labor: establishment of industrial armies, especially for agriculture;
9) combination of agriculture with manufacturing industries: gradual abolition of the distinction between town and country, by a more equable distribution of the population over the country;
10) free education for all children in public schools. Abolition of children's factory labor in its present form. Combination of education with industrial production and so forth.

I'll leave it to you to ponder which apply to America today, but as you can see, Marx characterizes the society as having a large, powerful central government whose power extends far beyond the mere "regulation of commerce" as called for in the U.S. Constitution. It wields the responsibility of *directing* the economy, not merely regulating it.

Although many have characterized socialism as a stepping stone toward communism, this is not reflective of Marx's and Engels's writings. I suspect it was the attempt to salvage the concept of communal ownership of resources and dissociate from the harsh implications of a highly powerful government, but the important thing is to squash the misconception now. As noted in *The Oxford Handbook of Karl Marx*, "The notion that 'socialism' and 'communism' are distinct historical stages is alien to his work and only entered the lexicon [terminology] of Marxism after his death."

Democratic Socialism: New!
Now Better -Tasting!

We now have a clear conception of Marx's view of socialism, but is that really what the democratic socialists in America are calling for today?

Again, another tricky term. As I discussed in the previous chapter, democratic socialists' tendency to describe the intended outcomes of their system rather than the policies of the system itself leaves many voters confused. However, a full press conference from "the Squad," as they're called, (Congresswomen Ocasio-Cortez, Rashida Tlaib, Ayanna Pressley, and Ilhan Omar) delivered one answer that best substantiates the term rather than muddles it.

> ...*[A] vision of humane social order based on popular control of resources and production, economic planning, equitable distribution, feminism, racial equality, and non-oppressive relationships.*

Seems...okay, right? One should note their invocation of the similar terminology we saw in Marx's definition of socialism, namely "popular control of resources," "equitable distribution," and "non-oppressive relationships." It's also worth noting the loaded language of a statement like this. "Equitable" is code for equality of outcome, another idea central to Marx's brand. More importantly, it's distinctly different from the capitalist notion of equality of opportunity. The two concepts are very different and should not be confused. The former focuses on outcomes, the latter on access, and they normally tend to grow at the expense of each other.

But it's important not to blur the lines between Marx's socialism and that of the Squad. The best articulation of this distinction comes from an unlikely source: right-wing author Dinesh D'Souza. In his work *The United States of Socialism*, he lays out a refreshingly fair-minded, nuanced description of democratic socialism. He rightfully highlights that socialists in America do not call for a government control of most sectors of the American economy, only...some. Their policy prescriptions involve the conversion of Obamacare to a national single-payer health care system of Medicare for All, a substantial increase in the minimum wage, the government provision of a universal basic income (UBI), free college, student debt cancellation, and last but not least, the Green New Deal. He also notes the universal call of socialists for extremely high tax rates on wealth.

We have to recognize that these policies only massively increase the control of government over the economic and social life of the population at large—never the opposite. So what are these policies supposed to deliver?

...And What Do They Want?

> *As long as our economy and political systems prioritize profit without considering who is profiting, who is being shut out, we will perpetuate this inequality.*
>
> —Congresswoman Ilhan Omar

Prominent voices like Congresswoman Omar point to socialism as the moral avenue of obtaining equality. This is hardly new. It is the embodiment of an old and rudimentary understanding of equality. Cries of "economic injustice" might prompt one to question what exactly constitutes such an act? Is it theft or cheating? No. It is the mere existence of economic variation itself. Martin Malia, the UCLA professor and expert in Russian history I mentioned earlier, knew this well. He articulated such understandings of socialism brilliantly.

> For if one is ruthlessly logical about the idea of democracy as equality, then one inevitably arrives at the concept of socialism. So long as there are differences of wealth in society, there will be differences of power and status; and so long as there are differences in power and status, there will be exploitation of some men by others, and domination of some human beings by other human beings. But exploitation and subordination are a denial of human dignity, a profanation of the sacred persona of man. Inequality, therefore, is dehumanization, and thus a moral scandal that must be ended if the world is to become truly civilized. The means to do this is through the social appropriation of individual wealth, and this is the core instrumental program of integral [or full] socialism.

It's not entirely wrong at face value.

Understanding equality in such terms may be reasonable to a degree. Undoubtedly, money is, by many estimates, an essential stepping stone for gaining political power. In 2012, the average cost of a successful congressional campaign totaled over $1.5 million, but this is not the full story. God's gift to America, former mayor Mike Bloomberg, spent over $900 million of his *own* money on his bid for the 2020 presidency. To put this into context, that's roughly the cost of 107 yachts. He dropped out of the race without winning a single state. Like a lab-constructed control experiment playing out in real time, Bloomberg curiously proved to America that even virtually limitless money can't secure all power.

In this spirit of concern over the unequal distribution of money, democratic socialists claim the end result of their policies will be a democratization of the economy. They say they want to help the little guy. Shouldn't we all want this? Let's first question the implications of pursuing, as Malia put it, "the social appropriation of individual wealth." Let's take a look at three policy proposals common to the democratic socialists to understand their means of democratizing our economy. If such policies truly promote economic democratization, they merit, at the very least, our consideration. Consider three of the most popular democratic socialist policies.

First, they call for a substantial increase in the minimum wage to a "living wage." The price tag? Fifteen dollars an hour. It doesn't sound too crazy at all. Set aside the question of whether this policy would actually work in lifting people out of poverty for just a moment and consider *what percentage of U.S. workers actually earn minimum wage?*

The way democratic socialists talk about it, you might think the threat of low minimum wages was a common, serious threat to the everyday family. As Senator Sanders put it, "We were told that raising the minimum wage to fifteen dollars an hour was 'radical'…but *millions* of workers throughout this country refused to take 'no' for an answer." One minor problem: There aren't millions of workers earning minimum wage or less in the United States. There are some, of course, but they only constituted a mere 2.1 percent of the total U.S. hourly workers in 2018. This represents a substantial decrease from the 13.4 percent they constituted in 1979.[2]

More importantly, a huge bulk of these workers are *not* supporting families. They are teenagers and college students. The U.S. Bureau of Labor Statistics found that those under twenty-five "made up just under half of those paid the federal minimum wage or less." Only 1 percent of the total share of minimum wage earners work full time.

So forgetting the question of whether higher minimum wages actually help the poorest of the poor—plenty of studies indicate they don't—we see that this hypothetical picture of millions of families subsisting on a minimum wage isn't accurate. An incredibly small, decreasing portion of the hourly U.S. workforce actually earns this much, and a huge portion who do are just beginning their journey in the job market. So why are the socialists harping on an issue that widely isn't an issue? We'll touch on this later.

Second, socialists want student debt cancellation. Friendly reminder that when talking about "the means of production," it's not unreasonable for money to fall under this category. It's hard to produce much of anything without money to start with, unless, of course, you're an author with no money at all.

Not sure what that's like. Nevertheless, back to student loans. Congresswoman Rashida Tlaib, who personally owes over $50,000 in student loans according to *Forbes*, said, "Canceling student debt is a racial justice issue...lower-income earners, especially black and brown people, have higher balances and are more likely to leave school because they can't pay."

I'm not going to say how anybody should feel about that statement, but personally, I'd take offense if a similar statement were made about women. Imagine. "Canceling student loan debt is an issue of feminist justice because women largely can't pay back their loans as low-income earners."

I'm willing to concede this would help some people on the bottom, but it would certainly hurt others. I've been a college student, and I know what it's like to have $3.26 to your name. Not so much fun. But I think it's worth asking which people on the bottom this would help. And who would be footing the bill? Yes, some would benefit, but does that make it right? These are the hard questions that make tempting policies less appealing under closer analysis.

Heck, for this one, I'll even concede good intentions. It's fun to be generous with other people's money. But good intentions aren't always good policy. Student loan cancellation proves a severe moral wrong on two separate accounts. First, who took out the loan? Even if colleges are charging way too much (which they are) and lenders may offer predatory deals (which they do), students voluntarily enter into these loans. They sign on the dotted line and take the money. Giving students a Get Out of Jail Free card is hardly the responsible or ethical answer for a voluntary loan. Second, who now has to pay it? As commentator

Matt Walsh once pointed out, there is no such thing as student debt cancellation; there is only *transference*. Someone *will* pay for the loan. Be it the original lenders, the taxpayers, or some other unfortunate bloke, the loan *will* be paid for. It's simply a matter of *who*. Most importantly, this is a solution that doesn't solve the root of the problem, setting an unsustainable precedent and an unfair abandonment of responsibility for costs.

But Wait, There's More: The Green New Deal

Finally, the newest sight of our socialist eyes presents perhaps the most significant threat to economic liberty in my lifetime: the Green New Deal (GND). While the name fosters green new feelings that we can save our "dying" environment, the content reveals different motives. This is no secret; you can Google the pdf and read it for yourself. It flows more like Marx's newly discovered Christmas wish list than a serious plan to solve climate change. The proposal calls for "guaranteeing a job with a family-sustaining wage, adequate family and medical leave, paid vacations, and retirement security to all people of the United States."

But wait, there's more!

The GND also calls on the federal government to "[provide] all people of the United States with high-quality health care; affordable, safe, and adequate housing, economic security, and clean water, clean air, healthy and affordable food, and access to nature." You might rightfully be asking yourself what any of this has to do with saving the environment. The answer is *absolutely nothing*, but don't take my word for it. Saikat Chakrabarti, former chief of staff to Congresswoman Ocasio-Cortez, is on record saying, "The interesting thing about the Green New Deal is it wasn't originally a climate thing at all. Because we really think of it as a how-do-you-change-the-entire-economy kind of thing."

Take note. These are the mask-slips we have to take seriously. In moments like this, they're saying the quiet parts out loud.

The reality is, Chakrabarti is absolutely right. This isn't *really* about the climate. If it were, it wouldn't be running to renewables with arms wide open. Since Germany has embraced their vision of full reliance on renewables, their emissions have gone up, not down. Even back in 2016, experts were telling us renewable energy density was far too low. The idea of fully relying on the source for twenty-first-century energy consumption was, we were told "an appalling delusion." This proposal rings the bells of climate alarmism to scare the American people into accepting a green new socialism, and it's working. A 2019 poll found that of American adults, 63 percent approve of the GND More disturbingly, 60 percent of *registered voters* support it. While it might be safe to assume most of these voters have not actually read the bill and simply wish to support measures to protect the environment, it only highlights the massive deception taking place. It is precisely this type of two-faced legislative underhandedness we should be leery of.

Apart from the totally unrelated socialist honey-do's in the proposal, more evidence shows the dubious nature of the supposedly nature-friendly bill. In addition to a supplementary document that outright condemned nuclear energy (later retracted), the bill makes *no mention whatsoever* of what President

Obama called, "our largest source of fuel that produces no carbon emissions": nuclear energy. To her credit, Representative Ocasio-Cortez later clarified that the proposal "leaves the door open" for such sources, but such retroactive ameliorations are, in my opinion, paltry at best. A solution that entirely ignores our greatest avenue to environment-friendly energy can hardly be taken as a serious solution at all.

So What's the Point?

What are these socialists up to? They claim to represent the little guy, uplift the poor, and save the environment, but the policies they propose hardly produce these effects. I think we have to dig a little deeper to understand the driving forces behind these deeply ideological pulls in our country. When Ocasio-Cortez says, "You have a right to a job, a right to an education, a right to a dignified home, a right to a dignified retirement, and a right to health care," should we even believe the government has the ability to provide us with these things? And where is that in the Bill of Rights?

Real concern over serious problems has historically proven a circumstantial sweet spot for power-hungry individuals.

Moreover, we know that when it comes to calls for concentrating power into the hands of a few, only the rank and file of the movement actually believe in the cause at hand. Hannah Arendt, an insightful writer during the twentieth century, interviewed the Nazis prosecuted during the Nuremberg trials (which were an absolute failure in delivering justice, but that's beside the point). During these interviews, she found a distinct pattern within the ranks of the soldiers: the lower the ranking of the Nazi, the more he actually believed in the cause. He recited the slogans, believed in the movement, and did everything in promotion of his belief in the Third Reich. However, as the ranking of the individual Nazi increased, he believed proportionately *less* in the actual cause of the movement and was far more concerned with the simple securing of *power* for the ideological party. The movement be damned. Power was the ultimate goal.

I believe the same rule applies to ideological socialism.

To account for any possibility of misrepresentation, let me make this clear: I am *not* comparing socialists with Nazis. I'm simply highlighting that power grabs are unstable long term without an ideological movement to support them, and normally it is only the people at the bottom who care about the simplified slogans of the movement itself. Those at the bottom supporting the movement believe "we need a Green New Deal," "health care is a human right," and that everyone deserves a "living wage." The followers are invested. They're all in. But based on the policies the socialist leaders propose, it's not really about helping those at the bottom. The people nearer the top secure power above all else. The movement be damned.

But even if it were the case that the masterminds of socialism in America truly want to help the poor, which I do not believe it is, the very population they claim to advocate for are the very population their ideology simultaneously belittles and demeans. I cannot underscore how unmistakable this disparagement truly is, and this should come as no surprise.

The Marxist line of thinking from which their viewpoint descends has always viewed the working class this way. "By the acts of modern industry, all family ties among the proletariat are torn asunder [apart], and their children transformed into simple articles of commerce and instruments of labor."[3] You see, as part of the working class, by default, you are incapable of treating your children as anything other than economic means to an end. Beyond that, all the lowlifes that comprise the proletariat can't even hold patriotic sentiments. Marx claimed, "The workingmen have no country. We cannot take from them what they have not got."[4] This underlying condescension toward the working class was true then, and it is true now.

Socialism, in any form, is equally and undeniably rooted in disdain for working class people, the proletariat. They don't think poor people are responsible enough to pay back the loans they take. They don't think poor people are capable of making a decent living for themselves on their own. Bottom line: working-class folks are seen as a liability to account for, not an asset to embrace. Socialism rejects the idea that free people can morally and effectively determine the outcomes of their own lives. Rather, government control is needed to both determine and secure the outcomes and welfare of the lives of all, not just the proletariat.

Admittedly, the democratic socialists' proposals in American politics today are not as extreme as the solutions called for by Marx. It would be dishonest of me or anyone else to suggest they are. Senator Sanders is not calling for the nationalization of agriculture. Representative Ocasio-Cortez is not suggesting a government seizure of private land for public use. Although the solutions they suggest are different from those of Marx, the ideology that guides them is very much the same.

The similarities are hard to miss.

First, look at the adversarial narrative of both ideologies. Marx viewed the nobility as the cause of the oppression and struggle in the working class. Democratic socialists likewise invoke a highly racialized fusion of identity politics, critical race theory, and diluted socialism. Native-born, white, male, straight, cisgender. The more boxes you tick, the more likely you have inherited your lot through oppression. Is it any wonder white males are the leading demographic for suicide? These narratives certainly are *not* responsible for this outcome, but they hardly help the situation either. Open vilification of certain groups does not lead anywhere good.

The Gulag Archipelago showed us this. In Aleksandr Solzhenitsyn's harrowing account of brutality under the U.S.S.R., he showed us that the deep temptation of assigning evil to one group *came in its removal from our own identities.*

> *If only there were evil people somewhere insidiously committing evil deeds, and it were necessary only to separate them from the rest of us and destroy them. But the line dividing good and evil cuts through the heart of every human being. And who is willing to destroy a piece of his own heart?*

If the bad guys are the source of all evil, we remove such assessments from ourselves. It becomes easy to see why, perhaps, the eradication of evil in the form of *that group* could possibly be necessary. It's a dangerous thought path, and it's one we don't want to follow.

Admittedly, Senator Sanders of all socialists has stepped away from this more racialized political perspective, but I can't help but speculate that he does so because the cards are not stacked in his favor…all that maleness, all that whiteness. This new metanarrative of the oppressors and the oppressed has been drawn along stark, disturbing racial and class lines. Such collective, simplistic terms of viewing our economy, history, culture, and politics have proven historically disastrous, which I will explain in a moment. They are the standard foreshadowing of terrible atrocity to come. We have to recognize such dangerous collectivized narratives for the threat they are.

Second, both ideologies justify the forcible seizure of another's property as the way to satiate and rectify these oppressor/oppressed dynamics. We're not talking about punitive fines for stealing or the specific repayment for a contract violation. We're talking about forcible reallocations of wealth totally devoid of any specific preponderance of individual innocence or guilt, the "redistribution of wealth." While I will go more in depth on this later, calls for reparations are the most prominent example of such thinking. Likewise, numerous calls to specifically cater to certain racial groups repeatedly appear in the Green New Deal.

This obvious line of thinking can clearly be identified in Marx's writings and the actions of democratic socialists today. "Of course, in the beginning this [establishment of socialism] cannot be effected except by means of despotic inroads on the rights of property and on the conditions of bourgeoisie production," Marx wrote nearly two centuries ago.

Today, democratic socialists are using just those methods. The Make Billionaires Pay Act proposed by Senator Bernie

Sanders and democratic Senators Ed Markey and Kirsten Gillibrand, would have slapped billionaires with a one-time 60 percent tax on all wealth gains made between March 2020 and January 2021. They intended to use the reclaimed wealth for the out-of-pocket health care expenses for the rest of America during the pandemic. Unreal. Thankfully, this legislation never passed, but it sets an incredibly disturbing, brazenly Robin Hood-like precedent.

Look, I'm just as concerned as the Democrats are about the massive funneling of business to corporate conglomerates during the pandemic. That's seriously concerning for mom-and-pop shops. The lockdowns were a hard, potentially *bad* idea, and they hurt small businesses the most. But entrepreneurs Jeff Bezos and Elon Musk are not at fault for the government threatening to put people in jail for doing business. In fact, businesses like theirs hired tens of thousands of people when millions were out of work. A referee can't kick the legs out from under one player and then take thirty points away from another. The first injustice of the lockdown was wrong in many ways, but it didn't justify a second punitive injustice on those who didn't inflict the first.

The ideology of both the original socialists of the nineteenth century and the democratic socialists of today is one of similar envy, entitlement, and unfairness rooted in collectivist, adversarial narratives. Americans haven't trusted it in the past, and we certainly shouldn't trust it now. I could go on about the expansion of a government people don't trust. I could talk about the realization of various mob-rule injustices our Founding Fathers tried to protect against in a federalist system of governance.

I could even talk about the embarrassment of democratically adopting a historically failed economic system. The routes of attack against socialism today are profound and plentiful, but none is more damning than the history of the twentieth century.

Round 987,610,876 of the Failed Experiment

One in three millennials views communism favorably. One in five thinks meh, what the heck, do away with private property! Over half believe *The Communist Manifesto* better ensures freedom than the Declaration of Independence. Whatever comforting distinctions leftists try to make between socialism and communism should ring hollow with statistics like these. Young people want Marxist policies no matter which way you slice it.

As the daughter of a public school teacher, it pains me to say it, but the American education system (except you, Mom) has *failed* my generation. Over 60 percent of millennials and Gen Z adults don't know that six million Jews were murdered in the Holocaust, and 11 percent believe the Jews actually *caused* the Holocaust. To say we're lacking historical literacy on twentieth-century issues is like saying President Trump is a narcissist: it really goes without saying. The problem is, that's the century where the vast majority of socialist regimes took place.

This educational failure poses a huge threat to America as we know it.

I know where you think this is headed, and I can tell you're already bored. "Those who don't learn history are doomed to repeat it," and education is the path to the future, and blah, blah, blah, blah. The pattern that emerged from the twentieth century proved the exact opposite. Of course education is important, but sometimes reality is too complex for the clichés to capture. As far as socialism is concerned, those who do know the history all too often excuse it, deny it, and misrepresent it.

Educated, intelligent people *can* repeat history, and they *do* repeat history. Often.

A widespread lack of education on basic historical knowledge is obviously a problem, but it is certainly not the only one, or even the main one. Knowledge matters, but it's useless without honesty to guide it. When it comes to the history of socialism, our biggest obstacle is not ignorance. It is dishonesty.

The Bad Idea That Refuses to Die

If there were an award for the idea most immune to overwhelming historical and humanitarian refutation, socialism would win. By a landslide. You don't have to take my word for it. Dr. Kristian Niemietz, director of political economy at the Institute of Economic Affairs, captured both the historical and psychological pattern of denial about socialism in his book *Socialism: The Failed Idea That Never Dies*. In a recent interview with *Forbes*, he discussed how the twentieth century saw over two dozen failed socialist experiments.

> *It has been tried in the Soviet Union, Yugoslavia, Albania, Poland, Vietnam, Bulgaria, Romania, Czechoslovakia, North Korea, Hungary, China, East Germany, Cuba, Tanzania, Laos, South Yemen, Somalia, the Congo, Ethiopia, Cambodia,*

Mozambique, Angola, Nicaragua and Venezuela,
among others—not counting the very short-lived
ones. All of these attempts have ended in varying
degrees of failure.

This won't stop another resurrection of Marx. The psychological gymnastics used to salvage this cancerous, failed idea follow a surprisingly predictable pattern. Dr. Niemietz shows how this pattern follows three universal phases.

First, much like an initial crush, Western intellectuals start out infatuated by the given emerging socialist government. Totalitarian or democratic, it makes no difference. This honeymoon phase is a rush of euphoria for leftist politicians and intellectuals. They're excited to see the ascendency of a "democratic, inclusive economy," as they like to call it.

How about a recent example? Senator Sanders rejoiced over Venezuela back in 2011. His senatorial page boasted, "These days, the American dream is more apt to be realized in South America in places such as Ecuador, *Venezuela* and Argentina, where incomes are actually more equal today than they are in the land of Horatio Alger. Who's the Banana Republic now?" This statement persists on his page to the time of this writing: October 14, 2020.[5]

Second, as the newly emerged socialist state's failings become more public, intellectuals enter what Niemietz calls the "excuses-and-whataboutery period." In this phase, intellectuals attempt to defend the socialist state by blaming the failures on external forces like foreign interference or capitalist instigators.

All becomes relative and definitively *not* the fault of the new socialist government.

Congresswoman Ilhan Omar fulfilled this phase to a T with her egregiously erroneous statements in May 2019. "A lot of policies that we [the United States] have put in place have kind of helped lead the devastation in Venezuela, and we have sort of set the stage for where we are arriving today." Ahhh, so *America* is responsible for Maduro's murder quotas fulfilled with the execution of his own citizens, *right*?

Finally, the leftist intellectuals enter their last stage of full-on denial. This is called the "not-real-socialism" phase, where the failure of the socialist state is so incredible and undeniable that they decide it's probably time to jump ship completely. Such condemnations are otherwise known as the "no true Scotsman" fallacy. It uses appeals to purity as a way to dismiss legitimate flaws in a position.

Truthfully, I don't think the American left has quite entered the third phase of this progression on Venezuela quite yet, but I'm confident they eventually will. The closest indication I found came from none other than Nobel laureate and economist Paul Krugman. He lamented via Twitter on February 25, 2020, "The real story is a lot more complicated than 'Sanders wants America to have a socialist regime like Venezuela.' No, he doesn't. But he has laid himself wide open to that kind of smear." If by smear, you mean taking direct quotes from his online Senate page, then yes, he should probably be worried about that.

Socialism is working, yay!

Well, that's not socialism's fault…

That was never even socialism to begin with!

Like clockwork, we can expect the same praises, deflections, and denials from leftist thought leaders as socialist governments play with human lives like rats in a lab. This Orwellian reconstruction of reality happened throughout the twentieth century, and it's playing out before our eyes in real time. We'll miss it if we don't pay attention.

Human lives depend on us not repeating this same mistake.

Americans are often stereotyped as an arrogant, condescending people who think they know better than everyone else. Embracing socialism would only prove such opinions are exactly right. Marx did not distinguish between communism and socialism. We can split hairs about terminology until the end of time, but ultimately, we're talking about Marx-inspired collectivist economies that killed roughly one hundred million people in the twentieth century. Translated into English and published by Harvard, *The Black Book of Communism* documents these atrocities in the forms of genocides, man-made famines, forced labor camps, political executions, and more. Other systems of governance are not without violence, but none come close to rivaling the body count of socialism.

For those still inclined to evoke some defense of Marx's ideology, I will leave you with a final word from Dr. Jordan Peterson.

> *When the Marxists say, "Well, that wasn't real Marxism," what it really means, and I've thought about this for a long time, it's the most arrogant possible statement anyone could ever make, it means "If I would have been in Stalin's position, I would have ushered in the damn utopia instead*

of the genocidal massacres because I understand the doctrine of Marxism and everything about me is good."...Well, think again, sunshine. You don't understand it. You don't understand it, and you're not that good. If the power was in your hands—assuming you had the competence, which, you don't—you wouldn't have done any better, and even if you had there would have been someone else waiting right behind you to shoot you the first time you actually tried to do anything good.

CHAPTER 3

AN IMMORTAL FAITH

[A]fter seventy years of experience with socialism, it is safe to say that most intellectuals...remain... unwilling to wonder whether there might not be a reason why socialism, as often as it is attempted, never seems to work out as its intellectual leaders intended. The intellectuals' vain search for a truly socialist community...results in the idealisation of, and then disillusionment with, a seemingly end-less string of "utopias"—the Soviet Union, then Cuba, China, Yugoslavia, Vietnam, Tanzania, Nicaragua.

—F. A. Hayek (1988)

EVERY YEAR THAT PASSES, I become less convinced that eighteen-year-olds should be considered legal adults. At eighteen, I entered college wide-eyed and ready to take on the world. Despite my outward persona of a career-driven, independent go-getter, I always had a gnawing feeling that the only real purpose of my undergraduate years would be getting an Mrs. degree. No one told me it had to be that way, but I couldn't find a logical way around the reality that marriage and a family—which I wanted—would mean goodbye career and hello homemaking. While I planned to pursue my education as long as opportunities were available, I privately estimated my hypothetical future marriage would do away with my career.

And then I met *him*.

We'll call him Mark. He was tall, handsome, and a couple years older than I. I don't think he had any strong feelings for me initially, but I was smitten from our first study session. Mark was not just smart—he was a borderline genius. An integrated genius. His success knew no bounds, from his activism to his career to his educational achievements to anything else he touched. All his endeavors turned to gold because that's just the kind of person he was. I didn't just want to date him. I wanted to be like him.

We gradually began spending more time together in study rooms and around campus. The fact of his apparent interest in me felt like stumbling upon a winning lottery ticket. I couldn't lose what chance had given me, and I needed to cash it in as soon as possible. He was phenomenal, unreal, superhuman, beyond my wildest expectations, and I was going to do as much as I could to make things work. (Again, how are eighteen-year-olds considered adults?)

As we grew closer, one thing became extremely clear. He liked me, but he did not respect me. My time, my emotions, and my affections were as disposable to him as a dollar to a billionaire. This inconvenient reality was, of course, concerning but insufficient to deter me. His continued patterns of disrespect, disregard, and carelessness were a small price to pay for the future I *knew* awaited us. He was my husband-to-be. He was going to be the father of my children. Mark's continued allowances of time for me were proof that he *really* loved me deep down…he just wasn't sure of it yet, but all my confronting and pleading could never produce the apology I really wanted: changed behavior.

This unhealthy dysfunction continued longer than I would like to admit, and frankly, writing about this experience does not bring me a sense of vindication or one-upmanship. It's embarrassing. Despite what all logic and evidence indicated, I had a deep, enduring, irrational faith that this was the man I was destined to build my life with. No reasoning or rationality could convince me otherwise. *Faith in the hypothetical future annihilated the evidence of the present.*

Why am I telling you this? It's not because I'm bitter or because I have an axe to grind. Mark and I made our peace and parted ways long ago.

I am telling you this because leftist thought leaders have led too many young people to adopt a similarly irrational devotion to socialism. Much like how I viewed my potential future with Mark, they believe socialism can deliver a moral safe haven of equality, prosperity, and human flourishing. Against all evidence, all logic, all reasoning, knowingly or unknowingly, they have faith that a socialist future will produce something better—despite its harsh record of abuses. They're hopeful. They're optimistic. They're excited about what they believe the future can be. I know because I've been there. It's precisely how I felt about my imagined future with Mark.

This is not to say that everyone who supports socialism is fully aware of the atrocities behind it. Obviously, many are not. Most young folks could not tell you what country first tried socialism or the resulting consequences from that trial (it was the death of millions). However, those who do know history must contradict all reason, evidence, and logic to believe that socialism can produce any good—and they're leading others into that same trap.

Despite socialism's historical record of consistently and perpetually producing government tyranny, genocide, torture, starvation en masse, and a sweeping disregard for human rights, socialism is hailed as the way of the future—America's hope to redeem itself. The intellectual circles of the left and, consequently, the vast majority of my generation as well, have an unshakable, unmovable, irrational faith that socialism can produce a better future.

I say this from personal experience: *unfounded, misplaced hope is the most devastating kind.* When that hope lies not in a fragile relationship with a young college boy but rather in an economic system that could drastically alter the lives of millions, there's a little bit more at stake. We're talking about millions of people's lives. We cannot afford to get it wrong. Unfounded, irrational hope cannot be our guiding principle no matter how optimistic or comforting it may be.

This may all sound a bit crazy, but as we discussed in the last chapter, socialism somehow outlives its perpetual failures directly against all logic. Why is that? There's a bigger problem here than just dishonesty. There's an entire philosophy of craven emptiness beneath the continued cries to "Eat the rich." Starting in the 1960s, this life support for a dying socialist ideology reared its ugly head in the form of *postmodernism*.

The Inconvenience of One Hundred Million Murders

What sustains the never-ending cheers for socialism despite the astronomical body count? It just so happens there's an entirely new, growing philosophy that sustains and emboldens many who still favor socialism, and Dr. Stephen Hicks of The Atlas Society intricately traces this progression in his book *Explaining Postmodernism: Skepticism and Socialism from Rousseau to Foucault*, which I cannot recommend strongly enough.

The fact is, Marxist atrocities of the twentieth century were *deeply* inconvenient for the public and academic reputation of socialism in the West. From the mid-1950s into the '60s, this reputational crisis became inescapable. Dr. Hicks identifies two major catalysts for this overwhelming refutation of socialism. First, the brutal suppression of uprisings in the Soviet subordinate Hungary. Second, the worldwide dissemination of Khrushchev's secret speech. To be fair, Dr. Hicks gives it a cursory mention, but a third event merits substantial, if not equal responsibility for the downfall of socialism: the international publication of Alexsandr Solzhenitsyn's *The Gulag Archipelago.* Stay with me. We've got some history to go through.

First, in the summer of 1956, Khrushchev accidentally exposed the U.S.S.R. when a secret speech he gave to the Twentieth Congress of the Communist Party of the Soviet Union was leaked to the Western world via Israeli intelligence. In it, he warned against the dangers of a cult of personality by detailing Joseph Stalin's atrocities. According to Khrushchev, not only was Stalin a rude and abrasive personality, he was a murderous one as well. He detailed countless false accusations, forced confessions, brutal executions, and tyrannical abuses that Stalin inflicted on his *own* party members. The world took notice.

Second, in October of that same year, Hungarians grew emboldened following Khrushchev's criticism of Stalin. Exhausted by intense economic hardship and highly oppressive political rule, they took to the streets calling for emancipation from the Soviets and for democratic governance. Their uprising was met with swift, brutal eradication. The power of the Soviet empire slashed through the people like a sickle through wheat and smashed in those left like a hammer on nails. This Soviet-style Tiananmen Square showcased to the world that the brutality Khrushchev criticized had by no means died with Stalin. It was alive and well and ready to run you over with a tank once you stepped out of line.

Finally, almost two decades later, despite desperate Soviet attempts at prevention, *The Gulag Archipelago* was published internationally in 1973. Solzhenitsyn's earth-shattering firsthand accounts of unimaginable abuse dispelled any surviving question of the Soviet Union's benevolence, toppling the Jenga tower of whatever legitimacy socialism had left. It detailed the horrors of brutal slave labor camps and indiscriminate political executions. The Nazis weren't the only ones with concentration camps. The twenty million human beings who lost their lives under the direct orders and policies of the Soviet Union made the Holocaust look almost tame. Almost. But sure, Kim Kardashian, keep rocking that woke hammer-and-sickle hoodie.

These three critical events upended socialism's legitimacy in Western intellectual circles. Hard to get behind a movement when it killed millions everywhere it turned up. A few remaining leftist intellectuals tried to salvage socialism by attributing the brutality to Stalin's cult of personality. Perhaps it was a mere aberration and misapplication. The reason I point to *The Gulag Archipelago* as the final death of socialism is because it eliminated any possibility of attributing the responsibility of the horror solely to Stalin. By meticulously tracing policy, Solzhenitsyn placed such responsibility directly at the feet of *Vladimir Lenin*, leaving no wiggle room for Western socialists. If the first two events were gallons of water dumped on the fire, the third was the final stamping out of any surviving embers of hope for socialism in the West.

Changing the Rules

At one point in time, socialists and capitalists were merely opposing teams, but soon enough they wouldn't even be playing the same game. Rewind to 1959. Zoom into a model kitchen at a trade exhibition in Moscow. Nikita Khrushchev, the head of the U.S.S.R. at the time, and then-vice president Richard Nixon stand in discussion. Khrushchev challenges Nixon:

"Let's compete. Who can produce the most goods for the people, *that system is better and it will win.*"

It's a funny proposal given it sounds more like capitalism to let merit succeed and dysfunction fail, but anyhoo, the Cold War tensions were as lukewarm as could be hoped for. A long-term economic competition was of course preferable to short-term nuclear annihilation. Eventually, the world got its answer. Capitalism had won, but rather than take the loss, the socialists decided it was time to change the game. Similar to why I refuse to go bowling, they didn't want to play games they knew they were going to lose.

Socialism could no longer stand on its own two feet in a court of logic and evidence, but what if it didn't have to? What if the entire metric for assessing ideas could be shifted from one of evidence and reason to one of subjective feeling? If so, socialism could one day rise again to political and academic legitimacy, and that's exactly what happened. Again, I cannot recommend strongly enough Dr. Hicks's *Explaining Postmodernism: Skepticism and Socialism from Rousseau to Foucault.* It demonstrates this evolution in the damning light of political opportunism.

Time for a rule change, a game change. This new game was postmodernism.

Postmodernism is best understood in the context of its opposite: modernism. Modernism is the philosophical movement that resulted from the Enlightenment and has dominated the Western world for the past two hundred years or so. The

Enlightenment has promoted reason as our primary epistemology (how we know what we know). This principle of reason facilitated the wonders of science, technology, and modern medicine. In terms of our understanding of human nature, it has produced a broad range of undergirding principles, including individualism, capitalism, and liberalism. These dominating philosophical directives continue to shape our lives even—especially—today. It was precisely these demands for reason and evidence that delegitimized socialism in the first place. But not for long.

In the 1960s, postmodernism emerged from brilliant minds cynical enough to ultimately "will nothingness" as Friedrich Nietzsche put it. Michel Foucault, Richard Rorty, Jacques Derrida, and Alasdair Gray led the intellectual left to its current, most dangerous form. Instead of using reasoning to determine truth, reason was wholly rejected. The truth does not exist. Only my truth, your truth, lived experience. Social subjectivism and antirealism dominate postmodernism. It rejects the notion of an objective, observable reality as well as our ability to confront such a nonexistent reality. Moreover, it almost invariably calls for a collectivist understanding of human nature and, consequently, a socialist prescription for government and the economy. It is a philosophy of subjectivity and antirealism.

Postmodernism shifts the court of appeals for understanding the world. In a world directed by largely traditional, logical thinking, we reach truth through the exercise of reason, logic, and analysis of evidence. Postmodernism completely uproots that. According to its adherents, because the truth does not exist, your power to assert *your* truth is the only tool you have left to engage the world around you. Language becomes your ultimate tool to secure power. The truthfulness or falsity of your claims makes no difference. It is your moral feelings and subjective values which reign because they are supposedly deeper, more real than any flawed human reasoning. Various components of postmodernism gave life to the necessary conditions for socialism's unwelcome resurrection from the dead.

No Reality. The metaphysical orientation of postmodernism is antirealism. Nothing really exists but how we think about things—much like the saying "perception is reality." Postmodernism echoes that in a completely literal interpretation. There is no objective reality, only the sociolinguistic constructs that give the impression of reality. Thus, language becomes the ultimate tool for constructing human reality. Foucault helped show the origin of this madness. As he put it, "The intellectual was rejected and persecuted at the precise moment when the facts became incontrovertible, when it was forbidden to say that the emperor had no clothes."

No Truth. In the absence of definitive reality, truth no longer exists. All is subjective. I must again cite Foucault, who captured such sentiments with startling straightforwardness. "It is meaningless to speak in the name of—or against—Reason, Truth, or Knowledge." In the absence of these critical avenues to understand culture, history, human nature, or reality, postmodernism points to one ultimate force for humanity's use: power.

Only Power. The texts of the postmodernists show one distinct pattern throughout: a consistent return to the concept of power. If there is no reality or truth, reality and truth become the narrative of whoever has the most guns, whoever has the most power. No appeals to reason or logic need to be made. All that is needed is the ability to enforce *your* narrative through power over others. Thus, it is these narratives the postmodernists ultimately criticize. "Simplifying to the extreme, I define postmodern as incredulity towards metanarratives," said Jean-François Lyotard.

A Philosophical Crutch

The human will abhors a vacuum. It would rather will nothingness than not will at all.
—Friedrich Nietzsche,
On the Genealogy of Morality

The intellectual left is not a group of dummies.

As a matter of fact, they're ingenious minds with seemingly endless methods to promote their awful ideas. We should probably recruit them on the right. Think about it logically. If you keep losing at basketball (the court of logic and evidence), switch the game to soccer (the court of emotional subjectivity). See how well the six-foot-eight-inch giants fumble with a ball between their feet as you speed by them with your expert soccer dribbling and a top-corner goal. They won't even know what hit them. As an experienced lawyer once said, "If the facts are on your side, pound the facts into the table. If the law is on your side, pound the law into the table. If neither the facts nor the law are on your side, pound the table."

These intellectual games are much trickier to follow than athletic games. At least in sports, there are explicit visual cues to indicate the sport at hand: a soccer ball, a basketball, a hoop, a goal, a field, a court. The intellectual games are not so revealing. You show up at a debate expecting to engage with facts, statistics, evidence, and logic, but you find yourself utterly lost in a game of emotional appeals and character attacks you were not expecting. I've experienced it firsthand, and I can tell you it's nothing short of totally confusing, frustrating, and bizarre. I watched it happen when my economics professor debated my leftist forensics coach on a public stage. It was like watching two ships pass by each other without any real confrontation. One relied on evidence, the other on emotional personal experience. The two were playing very different games, and it was obvious to everyone in the audience.

Let me give you just two examples of where this movement reveals itself most obviously: college debate and Antifa. Ask any college debater what is meant by "burn the state" and they will likely be familiar with the term. "Burn the state" is a common, highly detailed, and often passionately argued case to quite literally burn society as we know it. I listened in astonishment to the same case from college students all across the country. In essence, "burn the state" captures an important sentiment in postmodernism: contempt for existence. It is hopelessness realized as arson. When Mercer and Texas Tech were in the final round of the debate championship in 2018, guess what case Texas Tech ran? *"Affirm the impossibility of meaning."* Reject all meaning because, after all, there is no truth or meaning. This is not a fringe idea held by skateboarding, pot-smoking, blue-haired losers. It's a growing mainstream philosophy being actively taught and perfected among the most elite educational circles in the country.

The second and most visual representation of postmodernism at work is the indiscriminate burning and looting by Antifa. Following the death of George Floyd, these thugs took to the streets to shatter Starbucks windows, loot Target, and tear down statues. Peaceful protests were hijacked by hopeless postmodernists. Skinny, pale twenty-somethings donned black from head to toe and wreaked appalling destruction wherever they went. There was no real cry for justice from these Antifa thugs. They had no pragmatic policy proposal to make right their grievances. Their actions made one ultimate motive unmistakably clear: destruction.

To be clear, postmodernism isn't wrong about everything. Its skepticism toward those in power is vital to understanding history and humanity. We would be wise to practice a little skepticism ourselves. The problem with postmodernism is that it takes things too far. It isn't the critique of incorrect narratives for a productive purpose of reaching a solution. It is the ultimate rejection of any narratives or any useful means to improve them. In this vacuum of meaning, anything goes. Apart from a drive to secure power, the only guiding principle is absolutely nothing.

Between a rejection of truth and reality, a drive for power emerges as the primary source for shaping reality. No philosophy could be better suited to the rise of socialism than the one that ultimately rejects the need for evidence, reason, reality, or truth. It reminds me of the mindset I had with Mark. Instead of an honest assessment of problems for the purpose of finding solutions, I acted however I wanted to secure what I wanted without any clear guiding ideas.

Postmodernism provides the ultimate avenue for the socialists to do the same. They don't need to confront the broken ideology, only ever push forward for a utopia that's always just a few executions away.

Socialism Is Humanity's Abusive Boyfriend.

We make excuses for him, rationalize his behavior, and quickly forget how he treated us. No matter how many times he winks at us with genocide, flirts through mass starvation, or woos us with rampant political executions, we keep coming back for the marital bliss that awaits us when we *finally* get it right.

CHAPTER 4

FREE MARKET
ENTERPRISE ON TRIAL

*It is important to remember that capitalism has
been the greatest driver of prosperity and opportunity the world has ever seen.*
> —President Barack Obama

ORRY, PRESIDENT OBAMA, BUT MUCH of my generation
would beg to differ. They're not so much concerned
about the material gains we've made as they are about
those potentially getting unfairly cut off from the benefits of the
economy. These are legitimate concerns. This chapter cannot
address all such concerns, but it aims to address at least a few of
the most common ones. Is free market enterprise (capitalism)
holding back black people, women, and the poor? On the contrary, we have every reason to believe this system can equip such

groups to rise up and overcome whatever challenges they may face. They already are.

Racism: If It's in Our DNA...

I don't pretend to understand the Bible in its entirety, and I wouldn't trust anyone who says they do. Much of it has confused me. Even with a pastor for a stepfather, I have a hard time understanding it. But one of my favorite stories in the entire Bible leaves, in my opinion, little room for interpretation. In Numbers, chapter 12, Miriam and Aaron begin criticizing Moses, their leader. They criticize him not because of his poor leadership, immoral conduct, or personal flaws but because he has married a Cushite woman, a black woman. God comes to them and rebukes them, striking Miriam with leprosy on his way out.

You have to admit, that's pretty funny.

The irony of the punishment is apparently clear: Her now-diseased skin turns a sickly white. The God of the Old Testament effectively says to Mariam, "Oh, what was that about melanin? See how much you like your light skin now." Poetic justice. You may not believe in or even like the God of the Bible, but you can't tell me He doesn't have a sense of humor.

I believe most Americans long for racial harmony and a death to the racist divisions that have marred our past. Many today reject capitalism because they believe it is a racist system that works against black people. I know I once did.

We often hear statistics of the stark income and wealth disparities between white and black households in the United

States and think to ourselves, *How could this not be racist?* After all, it was our first black president, Barack Obama, who told us "...the legacy of slavery, of Jim Crow, discrimination in almost every institution of our lives—you know, that casts a long shadow. And that's still part of our DNA that's passed on. We're not cured of it." It always astounds me that the democratically elected black president could look at the country that gave him a majority of the popular vote twice, the highest office in the land twice, and call it racist.

Nonetheless, Obama and many others today believe just that: racism *is* a part of our DNA. No matter the fact that the vast, *vast* majority of Americans today approve of interracial marriage (upwards of 85 percent)—a deep indicator of racial integration. No matter the fact that Americans fought the bloodiest, deadliest, most brutal war in the history of the country's existence to end the evil practice of slavery. No matter the fact that the Ku Klux Klan is an openly disdained, politically irrelevant societal pariah that consists of a literal 0.000009 percent of the U.S. population as of 2017: only 3,000 members[6] in a country of over 325.9 million people.[7] No matter that white approval of racially integrating schools went from 32 percent in 1941 to 96 percent by 1995.[8] Forget all that.

Let's assume you don't take any of that as particularly compelling evidence. Some won't, and that's okay. For some, the question of America's racism is not up for debate. I want to use what space I have in this tiny book to win the battles I think I can. If you already believe America is racist, I'm not sure I have sufficient space to convince you otherwise here. Let's assume for a moment that America truly is the racist society that many like President Obama perceive it to be.

> *If the government and society at large are against black people for no other reason than the immutable color of their skin, free market enterprise becomes more important than ever for black people.*

Think about it.

If the government hates black people, why the heck would government control of their resources ever be conceivably portrayed as a positive thing? If the government hates black people, wouldn't a massive government seizure of the economy be their de facto death sentence? How could anyone with an ounce of human decency ever think socialism would be a good thing for black people if the government that runs it is committed to their destruction? How can we give the racists more power to determine what resources, housing, food, health care, and other basic services black people should get?

If the government and society at large hate black people, free market enterprise becomes their best shot to rise above.

Think about it logically.

The talent, ingenuity, intellectual capacity, and entrepreneurial capabilities of black people have historically proven to be something people in America want, regardless of however racist they might be. Black people are some of our most highly adored athletes: Lebron James, Serena Williams, Steph Curry, Jackie Robinson. Black people are some of our most acclaimed artists: Beyonce, Jay-Z, Nicki Minaj, Usher, Rihanna, Lil Wayne, Michael Jackson, Aretha Franklin, Whitney Houston. Black people are some of our most beloved entertainers: Will Smith, Morgan Freeman, Dave Chappelle, Viola Davis, Oprah Winfrey, Denzel Washington. Black people are some of our most revered intellectuals and leaders: Thomas Sowell, Condoleezza Rice, Martin Luther King Jr., Frederick Douglass, W. E. B. Du Bois, president Barack Obama. Black ingenuity has given America and the world countless invaluable inventions, including the modern ironing board, the home security system, the three-light traffic stop, refrigerated trucks, the carbon light bulb filament, and the color IBM PC monitor.

So what's the point?

The point I'm making is that even if the whole of America is inherently racist, it has proven itself not racist enough to contradict *its own self-interest*. America is better off for having black people as a part of our country and has proven time and again that whatever racist sentiments it may hold are not great enough to reject the talents, services, and ingenuity of black people in our country. Our options of services and products in the free market economy are greatly enhanced by the voluntary contributions of black people, and to pretend otherwise would be foolish.

Free market enterprise alone allows small or disadvantaged groups to rise above the hardships and discrimination they may face *to create their own prosperity*. It is through the merit of their own hard work and self-application that they advance beyond the obstacles placed in their way. If America is truly racist, there could be no greater act of violence against black people and all minorities to deny them the chance to advance themselves on their own talent, merit, and hard work.

Please do not misunderstand this thought experiment. I am not arguing that no racism exists in politics or economics in America. There are still issues to be addressed. As long as humans are alive, the sad reality is that there will be some racism. The primary sense through which we experience the world is ultimately visual. There will always be some who choose primitive tribal fears and irrational hatred over common decency and mutual respect.

Perhaps one of the most egregious examples of such overt racial hatred was the Greenwood Massacre of 1921. During this brutal attack, the wealthiest black community in America burned. "Black Wall Street" was razed. Death estimates ranged from thirty-six all the way up to three hundred, and thousands of black Americans were left injured and homeless.[9] This atrocity marked one of the most disgusting and disdainful events to have ever taken place on American soil. To add insult to injury, *no* reparations were enacted to replace the lost value of over $30 million worth of property and assets in today's valuation. This is not even the full story. The Charleston church massacre of 2017 showed us such racial atrocities can still occur today.

To say racism is completely eradicated from any society would be an exercise in naivete. Of course there have been racists—there will always be. But that doesn't mean racism defines or even dominates America. We can and should strive for a future that emphasizes integrity and merit as the focus, not our immutable differences of race. Free market enterprise does precisely that. When applied correctly, it allows people to succeed on the premise of their own competence.

Even despite a history of hardship, black people are proving they can rise above and thrive in a free economy. Coleman Hughes, a black American columnist, writes: "Though it has gone largely unnoticed, black Americans have been making rapid progress along the most important dimensions of well-being since the turn of the millennium." In his article, "The Case for Black Optimism," he lays out the impressive data points showing this progress in just the last couple of decades. Here are just a few.

- From 1999 to 2017, yearly black-earned bachelor's degrees increased by 82 percent and yearly associate's and master's degrees earned *more than doubled.*
- With 37 percent of black Americans aged twenty-five to thirty-four holding a college degree, were black Americans their own country, their educational attainment would rank them between Germany and Spain.
- More than 60 percent of blacks report they are doing better financially than their parents.
- Acclaimed economist Raj Chetty found in 2018 that black women are outperforming white women of equal socioeconomic background on income rankings.

This is just the tip of the iceberg. Go read his article for more encouraging proof that things *can* and *are* getting better for black America. This progress merits celebration in its own right. In order to get closer to a world where everyone is treated fairly, we can only proceed to one where people can succeed because of the good they provide regardless of the color of their skin. We can only proceed toward free market enterprise. As

Thomas Sowell put it, "Capitalism knows only one color: that color is green; all else is necessarily subservient to it, hence race, gender, and ethnicity cannot be considered within it."

I wanted to understand this firsthand. I reached out to black business owner and dear friend of mine April Chapman and asked her to share her experience as an independent business woman in America. As a successful furniture store owner, she shared what economic freedom means to her. Her interview has been attached to the end of this chapter for organizational purposes.

Women's Progress. Period.

Shirley Chisholm was the first black woman to ever make a serious, public run for president of the United States. She ran in 1972 for the Democratic nomination, a mere eight years after the Civil Rights Act of 1964 was passed into law through the great efforts of Martin Luther King, John Lewis, and countless others. Needless to say, given the heightened racial tensions of the period, Shirley Chisholm faced a massive obstacle. During her run, she shared a surprising perspective. She said, "I have certainly met much more discrimination in terms of being a woman than being black, in the field of politics."

This period of history, roughly 1960 to 1975, is one historically perceived by folks on the left and the right as some of the worst years of racial tension and division in America. Some fought for civil rights for black Americans. Others fought hard against them. Even in this critical period of America's racial history, Mrs. Chisholm saw her womanhood, not her skin color, as her greatest barrier to political participation.

Important barriers to our access to political and economic equality, I believe, are rooted in inconvenient biology. The fact of the female menstrual cycle and the woman as the physical carrier of a child during the gestation period have long been massive barriers to women's progress.

For much of human history, women have struggled to maintain their presentability in the face of a continual obstacle: the menstrual cycle. In early biblical times, women were exiled from their camps during their monthly periods. From the workplace to public life to the more general functions of regular social activities, the menstrual cycle has been a massive obstacle to women's full integration into society. Although this may sound like a ridiculous proposition, to give just one example, there are girls in India right now who are unable to attend school on a regular basis because of their lack of access to and money for feminine products. Every year, twenty-three million young women in India have to drop out of school because they start menstruating. Lack of awareness, hygiene products, and accommodating facilities are not just keeping them out of school; they are threatening their health.

For the men reading this and wondering what the big deal is, I'll try to give an analogy without being too graphic. Imagine, just for a moment, that you completely lost control of your urinary system. Due to no fault of your own, you could no longer control when your body relieved itself, but instead of passing urine, you passed blood. Without proper accommodations for your hygiene and disposal, would you be willing to risk the embarrassment for a couple weeks every month? Could you go on about your daily life? Would you risk the possibility of publicly humiliating yourself?

Of course you wouldn't. You would stay home.

The social barrier of the inconvenient, unchangeable reality of the menstrual cycle has perhaps been one of the greatest historical obstacles facing women. The beauty of free market enterprise is the fulfillment of critical human needs. Profit incentive drives otherwise potentially unconcerned persons to invent the best possible solutions for critical needs. Who invented the recent, revolutionizing product of the sanitary pad? Mary Beatrice Davidson Kenner, a black woman from Monroe, North Carolina. She came from a family of entrepreneurial patent-holders.

Such feminine products, along with the evolution and perfection of indoor plumbing, have been the capitalist response to one of the most enduring and pressing needs of women. Feminine products have in many countries effectively eradicated one of the biggest barriers to women's full participation in society at all levels. Free market enterprise fosters sensitivity to the needs of the consumer, to the needs of women. This makes it an indispensable tool for fostering equality between the sexes through their use of such products as well as their creation of them.

Moreover, the unchangeable fact of women as the carriers of offspring during the period of human gestation has made not only sexual freedom but individual freedom difficult to establish. The ability to choose when to have a child was, for the vast majority of human history, limited to a woman's capacity

to choose when she engaged in intercourse. However, the innovation of the modern birth control pill allowed women to more
effectively choose when they have a child. That's a big deal.
That's a huge deal.

Women gained a massive extension of their sexual and
bodily autonomy with the invention of the birth control pill:
perfected and affordably mass-produced under free market enterprise. This tiny white pill prompted women to pursue higher
education at unprecedented rates. Harvard economists Claudia
Goldin and Lawrence Katz found, "The pill further reduced
the cost of career investment for women by serving to increase
the age at first marriage for a large percentage of young people."

The ability of a free economy to efficiently, effectively,
and affordably meet the needs of the general public, especially
women, is unparalleled by any other existing economic organization. To be pro-capitalist is to be pro-woman in the most
profound sense of the word. The innovations and technologies
that put us on equal footing with men come about in the free
economies capable of rewarding those innovations. To oppose
free market enterprise is to oppose the very economic system
that has given women the most freedom, independence, and
autonomy of any historical period. No pun intended.

Poverty: The Lie That Won't Die

> *Two hundred million Americans make less than
> $20,000 a year—that's 40 percent of our country.*
> —Congresswoman Ocasio-Cortez

Despite the fact that those were her words precisely, every single number in the above quotation is completely wrong. A quick Google search can show you that, but it doesn't stop politicians and academics from exaggerating and outright lying about the state of poverty in America today. One of the biggest critiques of free market enterprise is that it facilitates poverty and exploits the working class. The data on poverty and capitalism leaves no wiggle room. Free market enterprise stands as the unchallenged, unparalleled, unbeatable champion of poverty eradication. This is not an opinion. This is what the data points show. I'll present the American case here and the global case in chapter 6. If we want poor people to have better lives, we need to support free market enterprise.

In America

However, many might say that Americans are suffering under capitalism as wages stagnate and jobs become scarce. Such concerns deserve serious consideration and merit the attention they have garnered. I'm not opposed to creative problem-solving, but we must carefully consider our serious concerns now in light of our historical and global economic progression.

According to the U.S. Department of Health and Human Services, as of January 15, 2020, an American who lives in technical poverty lives off of $12,760 a year (for Hawaii and Alaska, that number increases to $14,680 and $15,950, respectively). As of 2018, roughly 11.8 percent of the U.S. population was living in this poverty.

Poverty itself is a profoundly subjective term.

We gauge poverty in different terms depending on what we're assessing. From this reality of differing objectives come two different methods of measuring poverty: relative and absolute. Relative poverty, generally defined as "a condition where household income is a certain percentage below median incomes," shows what kind of poverty exists within a specific society. Absolute poverty is generally defined as "a condition where household income is below a necessary level to maintain basic living standards (food, shelter, housing)." It shows us where poverty as a condition becomes an immediately life-threatening condition.

Keeping in mind the (hopefully) universal desire that people should not live in poverty, we must take into account the pragmatic differences between various kinds of poverty. One type means you have harsh living standards. The other type means you might die of starvation. Both are undesirable, but one poses a legitimate crisis. The former (relative poverty) is tragic, but it is not nearly the same as the latter (absolute poverty).

Under free market enterprise, America eradicated absolute poverty to less than zero percent.

This reality came under intense scrutiny with the release of a massively impactful study in 2013 titled "Rising Extreme Poverty in the United States and the Response of Federal Means-Tested Transfer Programs." The study claimed, in effect, that extreme poverty in the United States, defined as two dollars or less a day per person, massively increased from 1996 to 2011 as a result of the Clinton administration's welfare reforms. The study states, "We estimate that in mid-2011, 1.65 million households with 3.55 million children were living in extreme poverty in a given month, based on cash income."

The groundbreaking research upended modern conceptions of poverty in America and influenced politicians, academics, and intellectuals across the nation. How could this be? Something must be done! The only problem? The grossly misleading data used to calculate these figures on poverty.

Based primarily on Census Bureau statistics, the study did not account for the massive discrepancies between self-reported statistics (as found in the U.S. Census) and factual realities (as verified with Internal Revenue Service and Social Security Administration records). Now, this is not to say the sociologists responsible for the study were being actively deceptive or intentionally manipulative, but it does demonstrate that the picture they painted of poverty in America is largely inaccurate.

Beyond this, they calculated only income with cash inflow. This metric of understanding household wealth fails tests of pragmatic usefulness and academic precedent by nearly all measures. Former Amazon CEO Jeff Bezos technically only makes a salary of $81,840, but we sure as heck don't pretend he is middle class. Relevant sources of income and resources must be accounted for in order to give a realistic picture of people's material well-being. Doing otherwise gives inaccurate impressions of what's happening on the ground.

The beauty of intellectual inquiry, especially in America, is that there are no sacred cows. Sparsely will you find a study unchallenged, a theory uncriticized, or an argument unrebutted. As my favorite political analyst Siraj Hashmi puts it, "the list comes for all." However, in this case, it just so happens that the demand for the existence of poverty to promote a specific narrative out-weighs the actual existence of poverty in the United States.

In May 2019, Bruce Meyer of the National Bureau of Economic Research published his research paper titled, "The Use and Misuse of Income Data and Extreme Poverty in the United States." His research noted:

> *Of the 3.6 million non-homeless households with survey-reported cash income below $2/person/day, we find that more than 90% are not in extreme poverty once we include in-kind transfers, replace survey reports of earnings and transfer receipt with administrative records, and account for the ownership of substantial assets. More than half of all misclassified households have incomes from the administrative data above the poverty line, and several of the largest misclassified groups appear to be at least middle class based on measures of material well-being.*

After correcting the erroneous data and accounting for all government benefits, significant assets, and other relevant sources of income, the number of single-parent households living in absolute two-dollars-a-day poverty fell to less than zero percent.

Naming and shaming those who have utilized such fallacious poverty statistics provides no practical or moral purpose. We'd normally expect Harvard-affiliated sociologists to know which data and statistics are accurate, but mistakes do happen.

But we *should* be concerned that it isn't stopping the authors from amplifying this inaccurate picture. The sociologists who conducted the initial study, Kathryn J. Edin and H. Luke Shaefer, capitalized on its popularity and published a book entitled *$2.00 a Day: Living on Almost Nothing in America.* The book received the *New York Times* (NYT) distinguishment of "Notable Book of the Year" in 2015, and an NYT review as an "essential book" and a "call to action" that "belies all the categorical talk about opportunity and the American dream."

For all this talk about the immediate, pressing needs of the poor, guess which of the two research papers was behind a paywall? Predictable. In response to Meyer's paper, the authors of *$2.00 a Day* doubled down on their assertions rather than backed away from them.

On June 17, 2020, (less than three weeks before I wrote this chapter), Shaefer responded to the refutational study saying, "Using the most comprehensive dataset ever assembled linking survey data to administrative earnings and benefits data, Meyer et al find that the group that mirrors the one Edin and I describe in our book—reporting extreme low cash incomes but receiving in-kind benefits—experiences the very highest rates of material hardship of any they examine." Shaefer asserts this despite the fact that a mere perusal of Meyer's abstract makes clear the study is, at least in part, a refutation of the arguments asserted in *$2.00 a Day.* Meyer states, "An implication of the low recent extreme poverty rate is that it cannot be substantially higher now due to welfare reform, as many commentators have claimed." Even as recently as August 2020, Bernie Sanders's use of the thoroughly debunked stats boasted a ranking of "mostly true" on PolitiFact.

Once the picture has been painted, no one really wants to take it back. The story has been told. The retroactive corrections be damned.

Such studies offer revealing insights not only into the state of poverty in America today but also to the political and academic conversation surrounding the topic. While the demographic described was materially poor, to say they lived on only two dollars of resources a day painted a wrongful picture. A critical component of the desirability—or undesirability—of free market enterprise is the degree to which normal people within the system can build decent lives for themselves. Beyond the surface-level conversations of the prevalence of poverty lies a deeper critique that the economic system itself is designed to put down, and keep down, the poor. This narrative can and must be summarily rejected. Let me show you why.

You're probably thinking, *What about relative poverty?* Even if absolute poverty is gone, shouldn't we expect more for the wealthiest country on earth? Of course we should, and there is ample evidence to support that things are getting better for the poor. The economic prospects of the average American *are* getting better on *multiple* metrics. Michael Strain's work *The American Dream Is Not Dead* provides substantial reason to believe our economy is working for those at the bottom. Consider: wages for the average worker, when adjusted for inflation, rose 34 percent over the last three decades according to data from the Bureau of Labor Statistics. More than this, successive generations are doing better than their parents. He notes:

> *73% of Americans in their 40s have higher in-*
> *comes than did their parents...86% of today's*
> *40-somethings who were raised in the bottom*
> *20% have higher incomes than did their parents*
> *when they were in their 40s. This is particularly*
> *important since upward mobility from the bottom*
> *of the income distribution is what we should care*
> *about the most.*

More than this, progress is reaching the vast, *vast* majority of us. The greatest technological advancements of our time are not in the hands of just the few. They are in the hands of the many, and I'm not talking about cheap plastic crap, though we certainly have plenty of that. I'm talking about life-altering technologies that fundamentally alter one's quality of life. An astonishing 96 percent of Americans own a cell phone, and 81 percent own a smartphone. That's a massive increase in both information *and* communication. What about transportation? As of 2018, 91.3 percent of American households had access to at least one vehicle. More technology? In 2016, at least 89 percent of American households had a computer, making it a feature of normal life. Health insurance? As of 2018, an impressive 91.5 percent of Americans had some form of coverage. I could go on and on, but you get the idea. Things are not perfect, no. There is certainly room for improvement, but the reality is the *vast* majority of us enjoy the technological advancements of our time.

We also have reason to believe we can better our situation with even *basic* steps. As demonstrated by a recent study[10] from the Brookings Institute, normal people from disadvantaged backgrounds have a good shot at making a living for themselves in America's highly capitalist economy. The study showed there were three basic norms that paved the path out of poverty:

- Graduate from high school.
- Work full time.
- Do not have a child until you are at least twenty-one and married.

If you follow these three simple rules, according to the study, you have a roughly 98 percent chance of lifting yourself out of poverty and a 75 percent chance of rising into the middle class. Now, this study has often been misinterpreted as a sophisticated way of blaming poor people for their own state of poverty. Nothing could be further from the truth. No intelligent person would deny the fact that life throws unexpected hardships at us, many of which are out of our control. People get sick. Car accidents happen. Unexpected expenses arise. To advocate the three above-mentioned norms doesn't mean that everyone who breaks these rules is solely responsible for their own state of poverty. Nor is it to say that anyone who follows them is guaranteed a cushy life. Both would be absurd.

On the contrary, such rules pose a critical lifeline for young folks trying to escape poverty precisely *because* life can be so uncertain. In a world where hardships are the norm and tragedies expected, we should cherish every piece of data-backed wisdom on how to gain autonomy over our own lives and safeguard as best we can from financial hardships. Free market enterprise gives us the space we need to make the best decisions possible, and that's especially true in America's free(ish) economy.

Dominant voices on both the left and the right constantly feed us a narrative of doom, gloom, poverty, and decline. We certainly have serious problems, and the pandemic didn't exactly help. But this is not the full story. My generation and Americans at large rightly want everybody to share in the success of our economy, not just a few. The demographics of concern including blacks, women, and the poor show we have *substantial* reason to believe a free economy *is* helping them too. As Harvard professor and author Steven Pinker put it, "It's essential to realize that progress does not mean that everything gets better for everyone, everywhere, all the time. That would be a miracle, that wouldn't be progress. And there are definite threats to progress." To put it simply, we shouldn't let the perfect be the enemy of the good, and when we look at the full picture, things are good and getting better.

An Interview with April Chapman

Can you tell us about your background growing up? What did your parents do? Were they well off?

I was born in the Bronx, New York, and grew up in the urban context in the late '70s, early '80s. I considered myself middle class; I lived in the 'hood but didn't realize it. My dad was in law enforcement, my mom in civil service/law enforcement. They divorced when I was four; I had four siblings. From 1984 forward, I was with a single mom who had to do everything on her own. No one had much money or owned property. We were broke; you just didn't know it. There was no thought of generational wealth transfer; we were living from check to check.

I've had the entrepreneurial spirit since five years old, when we would sell stickers and Cabbage Patch daycare. Full-on enterprise.

My mom is not college educated. I was a second-generation high school graduate, and my parents graduated from high school as well.

What kind of businesses do you own? Was it difficult for them to get started up?

The current businesses I own and operate are not my first businesses. Initially I owned an insurance agency. It had nothing to do with race; you just had to pass the exam, and you could work wherever you wanted—as long as they'd hire you. But I always knew I wanted to work for myself. I've always had a can-do attitude.

After the insurance agency, I started a bridal show production company and started producing bridal shows with my best friend. Next was retail furniture and manufacturing furniture in Georgia, as well as health-coaching services to people.

What were the top two or three obstacles to getting your businesses going?

Well, the furniture business is very tight-knit. Money is difficult to come by, and they don't want to talk to you unless you have a viable business location and license. The big challenge is trying to get capital. I started by flipping used furniture, then used that money to invest in myself. After all, I had to get a website, a phone number, etc. But my color presented no barriers.

What kind of volume do your businesses take in on an annual basis?

The furniture business is the most profitable: it's been in business for seven years. The first year we didn't even break $300,000. The most recent year has been the highest-grossing year so far. If we continue on track this year, they will hit $1 million.

And I've published two books during the pandemic. That helped catapult my health-coaching practice; that brings in around $12,000 a year.

None of the businesses were difficult to start. We used the talents we already had. It wasn't hard at all. Anybody can do it.

If you could trade your businesses for a guaranteed living from the government, would you?

Absolutely not. I don't want anyone, including the government, telling me, "This is the most you'll ever be able to make. Thou shalt not blah-blah-blah." Putting limitations on me will stifle growth and creativity. I want the ability to rebrand.

There is not enough security in the world to trust the government. I don't trust the government. I like the freedom and the satisfaction of earning my own living.

Have you ever felt that racial discrimination has in some way hindered the creation and/or success of your business?

I want to contextualize the answer. The first thing is black v. white. It never includes other ethnicities. Racism has not played a part. People who have helped my business the most do not look like me. The ones giving me the success secrets have all been different. White people essentially have been my mentors and helped us grow our business—whites, Asians, Indians, Syrians.

In this industry, the furniture industry, the ones that have put up barriers and not acknowledged me are black. Other black people at furniture trade shows. They are very guarded with their information. Nothing other than their name, very standoffish. The people who have helped me the most are the ones who recognize our mindset and our work ethic. I want to help them. It goes across color lines. It is about green and that's it. They're willing.

One of the things that bars us from success is when we only want to service people who look like us. Niche businesses do exist, but that type of mindset can only go so far. You then might think your race is barring you. If you have a good product or service, people will pay.

What does capitalism mean to you?

Capitalism is the only economic system that allows creativity and human interest to flourish. Your own efforts fulfill your own desires.

To me, capitalism means that I can, that I have the automatic freedom to create and provide services and goods in the marketplace. It allows me to be the free, independent-thinking person that I am.

Capitalism is the economic system that rewards a little effort or a lot of effort. It bars against laziness and complacency. It prevents the individual from relinquishing their responsibility to someone else who doesn't have their best interest at heart. It's the only system that allows you to pass on generational wealth. Under a capitalistic economic system, you can leave a legacy for your children.

Most people would affirm that the socialist mindset is not sustainable. We cannot trust the wicked heart of another person. Relinquishing the power to the state works with a just ruler, but not otherwise, and don't want my life to be dependent on the goodwill of another.

How does it make you feel/what is your response when people say capitalism as a system is racist? Is there truth to that statement in your opinion?

Absolutely not. C. J. Walker was a millionaire. She provided a great product. It had nothing to do with the color of her skin. Capitalism is racist how? On what basis do you make this assertion? Oprah is capitalism. Bob Johnson. Black entertainment. Tyler Perry. If capitalism is so racist, you wouldn't have black Hollywood. It flies in the face of the racist narrative. We experience racism because the heart of man is wicked.

It doesn't mean everyone is nice and fuzzy; there are rude and disrespectful people everywhere. Don't cry about it. They don't need affirmation from other people, and it doesn't mean white people set the standard. I have too many examples in history of people who lived under real racism. There are no Jim Crow laws that bar you from the business choices you want to make. There is nothing stopping me. It is the best economic system regardless of what you look like.

What is it you're barred from doing because you are black? What are these barriers? You have to name them. Resale licenses are not withheld because of skin color. Bad credit means you won't get a loan, period. And no one, black or white, could get a loan during the recession. Commercial lenders always have very stringent requirements.

We want more wealth, and oppressed minorities *can* raise themselves up from poverty to a level playing field...not through handouts but through hard work. Capitalism gets a bad rap from people who don't understand the way it works. They only care that the check is good.

CHAPTER 5

FREE MARKET ENTERPRISE: THE MORAL CHOICE

In a capitalist society, all human relationships are voluntary. Men are free to cooperate or not, to deal with one another or not, as their own individual judgements, convictions and interests dictate.
—Ayn Rand

RECENTLY, I DISCOVERED THE FASCINATING and highly controversial phenomenon known as pedophile hunting. It is not a literal manhunt with shooting or any type of killing. No violence is involved. Rather, pedophile hunting is the preferred method of a select few freelance journalists in combatting crime within their own communities.

The journalists create false online profiles of underage girls or boys. Once messaged, they make clear their underage status and proceed to engage with the pedophile, responding as the underage child.

Typically, the pedophiles lead the conversations into highly sexual and explicit directions. After a while, they suggest the minor meet with them to carry out propositions. But when they arrive at the agreed-upon location, they are met with cameras and pointed interrogation from grown men instead of a vulnerable little girl or boy.

Depending on the hunter, the practice can have impressive results. After the encounters, the hunters post the footage and conversations online for all to see. The would-be offenders are publicly named and shamed. The screen-shotted conversations and recorded footage are also turned over to the police, who sometimes proceed with pressing charges. Convictions and arrests have been made through pedophile hunting that would not have otherwise occurred. The practice helps remove predatory men from our streets. Men trying to abuse little girls and boys as young as twelve are exposed for the predators they are.

Sadly, most will agree our criminal justice system has not done enough to protect children from the hands of predators. One in four girls is a victim of child sexual abuse. One in thirteen boys meets the same fate.[11] With this atrocity so widespread, who could possibly get angry about pedophile hunters getting these predators away from children and behind bars? Well, many people don't approve of the pedophile-hunting techniques.

Many see the method as "entrapment." Pretending to be a young child to tempt adult men into committing crimes, they say, violates the pedophiles' civil protections. Plus, they view the practice as sloppy and attention-grubbing vigilantism. The job of "catching the bad guys" is best left to the police, they say. Finally, the public naming and shaming can have unintended consequences. In the past, it has pushed some pedophiles to commit suicide rather than face the public shame of being exposed. It's a controversial practice with difficult implications either way.

Those opposed to the practice are of course not opposed to the protection of children; they have a moral critique of the methods. It's the same critique we've heard since we first discussed Niccolò Machiavelli in our tenth-grade lit classes: do the ends justify the means? If the end result is good (pedophiles are put behind bars), does that mean the process by which we get there is de facto justified (pretending to be a sexually exploitable minor to expose criminal intent)? While I have chosen a particularly controversial example to discuss the standard Machiavelli logic, it applies to any number of different scenarios. Is cheating justified if it gets you a better grade on your test? Is lying to your boss justified or perhaps even obligatory if it means protecting a coworker from losing their job? Is torturing terrorists in Guantanamo Bay justified if it yields information to protect American citizens? The list of similar examples goes on forever.

The fact is that we're often faced with the painful decision between the moral choice and the utilitarian choice. One lets us look ourselves in the mirror without contempt; the other gets us the result we want…or desperately need. The deeply difficult dilemma of having to choose the moral option or the utilitarian one has plagued mankind from its inception. However, free market enterprise offers a unique escape from such binary options of morality and utility. In building our economy, for once, we have a unique choice that is both the moral and the utilitarian option. We can get the best results all while playing by the rules.

Economy or Morality? You Decide.

When it comes to our economy, it's hard to know which metric weighs heavier in our policy-making. Do we choose the economy that is moral? Or do we choose the economy that gives us the best results? After all, we're talking about resource allocation, a literal matter of life and death. If Venezuela can go from the wealthiest, most prosperous country in Latin America to one with the majority of its population on the brink of starvation, perhaps we should tread carefully with our own economy. We cannot afford to be wrong on this.

The question of morality seems to be the one currently dominating the economic scene. When responding to some of her misstatements, Congresswoman Ocasio-Cortez countered, "There's a lot of people more concerned about precisely, factually, semantically correct, than about being morally right." While I think this is a weak defense, it seems to be one that a lot of young people accept today. *"Regardless of how it works, the economy should be moral"* seems to be the prevailing sentiment.

Conservatives are needlessly losing this argument on the economy. It is perhaps our weakest spot in waging the culture war for the heart of America. This system allows individuals—the private sector—to make their own economic decisions.

Within the confines of the law, it allows them to do with their resources as they please. Those who reject the morality of free market enterprise overlook the foundational principles that make it so…morally right.

Free market enterprise is based on the concepts of individualism, personal freedom, and noncoercion.

So how does any of this relate to the concept of pedophile hunting and Machiavellian ethics? It's actually quite simple. In a world where we constantly face the painful choice of the utilitarian route or the moral route, capitalism presents one of the few reprieves from such a dilemma. *Free market enterprise is both the moral and the utilitarian option.* For this chapter, we will focus on the measures of *individualism, personal freedom, and noncoercion* that make it the most moral economic system on earth.

All of Us, Individually

It's so painfully obvious that I'm not even sure it's worth saying, but every individual is unique in his desires, talents, abilities, and goals. Capitalism stands alone as the champion of the individual. Socialist economies elevate the needs of the collective over the needs of the individual. Not capitalism. It protects the economic rights and economic freedoms of every individual. Such measures are the necessary prerequisite for the success of the collective. After all, it was Ayn Rand who famously declared, "The smallest minority on earth is the individual."

We've often heard Adam Smith's now iconic metaphor of the "invisible hand," which directs market forces to meet the needs of consumers. But we don't often hear about what I like to call "the individual hand." It is the ability of each individual to pursue the business aims abilities best suited to his or her needs. If you want to swallow swords on a public stage for a living, you can try that. If you want to bake pastries for a living, you can try that. If you want to (insert legal activity here) for a living, you can try that. While there is no guarantee that your endeavor will be lucrative, there is a guarantee that you have the freedom to pursue your economic aims as you see fit.

I think Americans, including myself, often take this precious economic freedom for granted. As in the adage of making a fish see water, economic freedom is hard to notice when you've been immersed in it your entire existence. But such freedoms safeguard the individual's ability to develop his own talents, pursue his own ends, and pursue his own form of happiness.

To allow every individual to pursue the path that best suits him offers an autonomy unlike many experience today. No bureaucratic boardroom in Washington gets to tell you the career best suited to your abilities. No disconnected executive has the right to tell you how your time and talents are best spent for "the greater good." You, in and of yourself, are allowed to pursue the aims you deem most worthy of your short time here on earth. The number of factors we cannot control in our lives is staggering: parents, place of birth, upbringing, body type, race, and so on. If I can have the freedom to choose my own career, you best believe I'll fight to keep it. In a world where there is truly so little we can control, we must preserve what freedoms we have over the things we *can* control.

Personal Freedom

Stupid but serious question: Why do we hate slavery so much? Is it because of the violence involved? No single concept, not even war, seems to trigger such a universal and passionate negative response as slavery. Even those who have been through armed conflict will often admit that, under certain circumstances, when no other options are available, war may be necessary. Virtually no one concedes that slavery is "necessary." It is always wrong.

Is it because of the creation and abuse of power dynamics? Possibly, but that exists wherever government exists, wherever authority exists, and it's only the anarchists that want to fully abolish government. So what is it about slavery that so deeply violates our human conscience?

I believe it's a complete violation of personal freedom.

When humans are kidnapped, relocated, selectively bred, and forced into physical labor entirely contrary to their will, it is not merely their physical condition that has been attacked, but their condition as members of humanity as well. The total removal of any semblance of autonomy reduces a human to an animal, at least in mental and emotional terms. The loss of free will in sexual behavior, association, career pursuits, family-making, location, and much more beyond that strips human beings of their ability to function as full, dignified persons.

So if we're looking for a philosophical starting place to craft an economy, wouldn't that be the opposite of slavery? If we know one economic system actively violates human dignity, shouldn't we look for its opposite to craft our own economy? If slavery—completely opposed to human autonomy—is the worst economic system, wouldn't the best system be the one that most preserves it?

Free market enterprise is the most moral economic system because it preserves and protects, in the greatest manner possible, personal freedom.

Under this system, to the greatest extent possible, you have control of your labor, your resources, and lastly, your money. Such freedoms not are not only sacred to the dignity of every person, they are the necessary prerequisite for collective success and political freedom. This is not to say all market-friendly societies are politically free, but all politically free countries *are* necessarily market friendly. Milton Friedman demonstrated this in his writings.

We detest slavery because it strips the individual of all that makes life worth living and places it under the authority of another. Free market enterprise becomes beautiful, sacred even, because it puts many of our personal freedoms of choice back under our own personal control. Such freedoms include property rights.

Oftentimes when leftists hear "property rights," their immediate distaste is for millionaires and billionaires who have accumulated wealth to the point of near absurdity. But I would challenge you to think of the implications of such protections for the poorest of the poor. Food is property. Housing is property. Clothing is property. All of these basic necessities suddenly leap far out of reach for the poorest of the poor if property rights are not protected. The elite, the politically connected will more often than not find their footings materially. It is the implication of such rights for those at the bottom of the ladder that should grab our attention most.

The safeguard of property rights, stability of government, and a trustworthy judicial system are all hallmarks of a successful capitalist economy. Fairness, or perceived fairness, lays the bedrock for normal people to feel confident enough to participate in the capitalist economy.

By allowing private individuals to own and control the means of production, we expand both freedom and utility. People have the freedom to pursue ownership and production. That is not the case under socialism. Under free markets, incentive remains high for such resources to be utilized in a fashion that not only maximizes profit but maximizes utility.

Many rightfully critique that, "Sure, you're free under capitalism. You're free to starve to death." This perspective lends perhaps one of the most poignant critiques of pure capitalism: risk of failure. But to me, this critique is best solved for in capitalism's final claim to moral high ground: noncoercion.

Noncoercion

Ultimately, the greatest aspect of capitalism, in my opinion, is not the freedoms it lends us or the individual it exalts. It is its noncoercive nature that allows people to flourish with as little economic interference in their lives as possible.

Many will say capitalism exacerbates greed and rewards selfishness. But I have yet to see any evidence that capitalism makes people greedier than any other economic system. Greed is eternal. As long as humans exist, greed will follow. More importantly, greed is a force of power. It can push individuals, groups, and countries to act violently. It is the root cause of countless wars and genocides. But if greed isn't going away, what do we do with it?

Harness it for something good.

When people can only reap rewards through providing something desirable for others, it saddles the horse of their greed to the driver of production for the surrounding community. It aligns social and personal interests in the most profound manner humanly conceivable. It means that helping my neighbor, my customer, does not come at a personal cost to me but as a paycheck *to* me.

It means that instead of my interests and my neighbor's interests being diametrically opposed to one another, they are aligned in a symbiotic relationship that benefits both parties. This critical component of mutual alignment represents perhaps one of the most novel and counterintuitive revelations of the last two centuries: people can and often do flourish when they are allowed to trade, work, and live freely in the chaos of personal choice.

When individuals can pursue and cultivate their own abilities through rational means, they excel more often. It is this noncoercive nature that allows both buyer and seller to engage freely and productively in business with one another. When we eradicate the threat of violence from the business equation, market prices can be more clearly identified and shifted, helping foster human prosperity and well-being.

More importantly, free market enterprise maintains two central tenets of noncoercion antithetical to the institution of slavery. Ayn Rand paints these principles masterfully in *Atlas*

Shrugged: 1) Nobody has the right to make you live for them. In other words, you are no one's slave. No one but you has any inherent right to you, your labor, your resources, or your money without your freely given consent. 2) You don't have the right to make anyone live for you. No one is your slave. You own no inherent right to anyone else's person, labor, resources, or money without their freely given consent.

As we saw in the case of pedophile hunting, many see it as a potentially effective but immoral way to catch bad guys. Answering for both morality and utility is no easy task. We all want to build a fair economy that actually works. People need to be able to meet their needs without violating the rights and dignity of others. On the building blocks of individualism, personal freedom, and noncoercion, free market enterprise has built just that: a system for profound moral prosperity in both principle and practice.

CHAPTER 6

THE LEGITIMATE
CRITIQUES OF FREE
MARKET ENTERPRISE

A S I'VE MENTIONED BEFORE, FREE market enterprise (capitalism) roughly equates to satanism within the college debate community. They do not simply dislike or disagree with it, they despise it. Safe to say, it's not the favorite among college debaters. The shorthand term for a critical case against it is known as a "cap k," or capitalism kritik. A 2015 article from the Victory Briefs Institute said, "The capitalism kritik has become one of the most popular critical arguments run in both Policy and progressive LD [Lincoln-Douglass] debate."

Why is it so popular? Because it stirs up such strong emotions. Some have rightly viewed capitalism as a process great for making basic improvements initially but outdated in its current form. The thinking goes something like this: Capitalism may be good for taking the banana from green to yellow, but now it is taking the banana from yellow to rotten brown. We need something new. The banana now oozes injustice, inequality, and climate change, we're told.

Such sentiments are not entirely unsubstantiated. Issues such as climate change, inequality, and cronyism present legitimate threats to the environment, democracy, and economic progress. But the solution to the well-placed concerns lies not in abolishing capitalism, but in reforming it to a fairer, purer form.

Climate Change, Not the End of the World

What's the biggest lie you've ever been told? I'll bet you don't even know what it is, and I know what you're thinking. No, I'm not a climate change denier. The science on the matter appears pretty clear that humans alter the climate through their activity. That much may be true, but what are its implications? If you listen to AOC, you probably think the world is ending in twelve—wait, no, I think now it's only ten?—years from now, and if we don't cede all fossil fuel production to the government for an immediate halt, we're doomed. Dandy, huh? Never thought cow farts would be the death of us, and yet here we are.

Climate change is real, but the doomsday conclusions drawn from it are not.

So much of the confusion about climate change stems from the politicized nature of the issue. If one side says it will be the death of us, and the other side says it isn't real, how are we supposed to know whom to believe? Some might say, "Just listen to the scientists," but one of the many lessons we all have taken from the COVID-19 pandemic (I hope) is that politicians can and do jump to politicize science and data if it suits their interests. That goes for both sides. But what could possibly be a more powerful pretext for massive political restructuring than the imminent extinction of humanity?

It scares the living daylights out of people.

The answer to climate change is not the abolition of fossil fuels, the abolition of free market enterprise, or a reduction of people. With a rough sketch of some of the most relevant data and trends and some historical context, allow me to point toward a counterintuitive solution that might surprise you: more people and more free market enterprise.

When we think about climate change, we tend to detest the pollution modernity has produced and romanticize the "good old days"…whatever that may mean. I thought this way for a long time too. We think to ourselves, *If only we were riding horses and living in nature, we wouldn't have these problems like we do now.* But what really were the good old days? Were past practices really so much better for the environment than ours are now? Much evidence points to the opposite. History demonstrates the continuous human struggle to make life not only survivable but enjoyable, and when we regress to previous strategies to achieve these ends, the results tend to be worse—for both us and the environment.

Take, for example, Nepal in 2015. The tiny, landlocked country sandwiched between India and China relies heavily on gas from India as one of its primary energy sources. After Nepal's passage of a controversial new constitution, India effectively, if tacitly, placed an embargo on their gas imports. Additionally, with a recent devastating earthquake, Nepal's Chinese border was in a total state of ruin, preventing access to stored supplies. With an over 80 percent reduction of their energy source, the Nepali people had to revert to the more primitive method of burning wood to warm their homes, cook their meals, and fulfill other energy-pressing needs. But at least they weren't using gas, right? Well, not exactly.

The new demand for firewood not only put nature reservations and thousands of trees at risk of illegal logging, but also resulted in a less breathable, more polluted atmosphere. The *Nepali Times* noted:

> *The fuel crisis has also forced households in the valley and even restaurants and offices to burn firewood for cooking. Since it is a temporary measure, most don't have proper chimneys or ventilation. Smoke from firewood has made morning smog worse, and also increased the risk of indoor pollution.*

Additionally, I had the opportunity to interview a Nepali woman who experienced the crisis firsthand. Shreeya Singh told me, "We always had air pollution, but when we reverted back, or were forced to revert back, to using firewood and coal, there was a noticeable smog that surrounded the city in a matter of days. Because of the fuel crisis, we were using less vehicles, but we were burning even more wood trying to stay warm in the winter."

In his groundbreaking 2020 article "On Behalf of Environmentalists, I Apologize for the Climate Scare," left-wing expert environmentalist Michael Shellenberger noted, "Wood fuel is far worse for people and wildlife than fossil fuels." In the same article, he lays out the progression of energy sources he believes will help alleviate climate change: "The most important thing for reducing air pollution and carbon emissions is moving from wood to coal to petroleum to natural gas to uranium." Effectively, he is calling for more development on our energy utilization, not less. The beauty of free market enterprise lies in its ability to use the brainpower of the whole of the populace rather than the few. As our demand for energy increases for both necessary means of survival and superfluous means of enjoyment, our ability to tap into the talents and innovations of the many will be a critical component of getting there.

But perhaps you're thinking to yourself, *Well, even if it gets better, there are too many people on earth for everyone's needs to be sustained in the long run. We've already destroyed the planet and its resources.* This sort of fallacious Malthusian thinking not only presents a massively antihuman threat, it contradicts much of the prevailing data on the matter. For example, the Simon Abundance Index of 2020 revealed that the earth's abundance grew by 570.9 percent between 1980 and 2019. The study also found that during the same time period (minus 2019), "the average time price of 50 basic commodities fell by 74.2%," meaning the time needed to work for such products has fallen by nearly three-quarters. This points to the conclusion that "Over the past 39 years, every additional human being born on our planet appears to have made resources proportionately more plentiful for the rest of us."

The most valuable resource on the planet is the human mind, capable of transforming the useless into the useful and the scarce into the plentiful. Free market enterprise has allowed us to tap into our most valuable human resource unlike ever before, and the results are proving it's a good investment. As Buckminster Fuller put it, "Pollution is nothing but the resources we are not harvesting."

Our track record with the environment has not been great. Before electricity and liquefied petroleum, we used to kill whales to make candles to light our homes. Before the invention of plastic, we killed turtles and elephants to make various household items such as combs, piano keys, jewelry, and other hard, durable items. Today, we've replaced inefficient and harmful practices with cleaner energy sources and completely new artificial materials such as plastic. Given our massive population increase in the last two centuries, we should take hope from the fact that we're getting better and better at using our resources efficiently while minimizing our impact on the earth. Development is pushing us toward better, more efficient practices than we used in the past. Expert environmentalist Michael Shellenberger, the writer of the environmental crisis article mentioned above, notes, "Factories and modern farming are the keys to human liberation and environmental progress." More importantly, in his book *Apocalypse Never: Why Environmental Alarmism Hurt Us All*, he documents the many ways in which the climate crisis is no crisis at all and in fact represents a very manageable change to our highly adaptive species.

With deaths from natural disasters decreasing by over 99 percent in the last two centuries, our ability to survive the environment is stronger than ever before. With modern technology to warn us and modern infrastructure to protect us, humanity is better equipped now more than ever to face whatever climate changes and challenges may come in the future, and that's largely thanks to innovations produced by free market enterprise.

Income Inequality

I contracted COVID-19 in the summer of 2020. Apart from losing my sense of smell and feeling as though someone had blown up water balloons in my nasal passageways, I got through just fine. Even though I try to wear them when appropriate, I must confess, I detest masks. With all the changes, I think most of us can identify with the feelings of exhaustion, frustration, and, for some, grief amid the pandemic hardships. I hope that has changed by the time this book reaches you. Every time I hear a commercial, public official, or school administrator babble on about our "new normal," I cringe with aggravation and despair at my powerlessness over my own ability to breathe unhindered in public places or control any of the craziness of this depressing, unhuman, artificial, and dystopian headache that has replaced reality. If there were ever a trigger for an internal dialogue full of furious disdain and suppressed rage, for me, it's hearing someone mention our new normal as if it were…normal.

"Income inequality" seems to be the new normal of the socialist left. The very idea of it angers them. As we discussed in chapter 1, the ruthlessly logical assessment of eradicating inequality is ultimately a motivation for socialism. "Income inequality" seems to set off some internal alarm that the unacceptable has now been identified and attack mode has consequently been activated. But why? It's not like there has ever existed a society where everybody has held the exact same amount of wealth, and even if it did, its very existence would necessitate a totalitarianism so encompassing as to make such "equality" itself altogether negligible to its insurmountable cost.

First, it's important to note the traceable roots of the conversation on inequality. Before socialists critiqued free markets on inequality, they contested the issue of need. "Capitalism fails because it doesn't provide for the needs of the poor" was roughly the prevailing contention. Three undeniable realities eviscerated this argument as the twentieth century progressed: 1) the plight of those living within capitalistic societies was not only good, it was exceedingly prosperous; 2) socialist and communist countries that consistently facilitated tyranny were collapsing one after another, leaving nothing but bodies, abuses, and barrenness in their wake; and 3) these two previous realities gave rise to the trend we see even today of people leaving socialist and communist countries in large numbers for the chance to carve out their own prosperity in the capitalist societies supposedly so incapable of providing for their basic needs.

As documented by Stephen Hicks in *Explaining Postmodernism*, these embarrassing realities forced the socialist left to switch their focus to inequality as the most pressing abuse of capitalism. Since absolute poverty had been often eradicated wherever capitalism was practiced, the new pressure point would be relative poverty. Wherever it could be found, it would be magnified.

> *A psychological bug was thus to be placed in the*
> *ear of every working American: having a white*
> *picket fence, the American dream, was no longer*
> *acceptable; instead it was to have the same wealth*
> *as your neighbor, i.e., equality. Similarly, some*
> *leftist intellectuals also turned to agitate women*
> *and ethnic minorities about their lack of parity in*
> *wealth to men of European descent.*
> *—Pocket Guide to Postmodernism*

Keeping up with basic needs to survive had long since become a thing of the past. It was now time to keep up with the Joneses. The question of the socialist left's initial and legitimate concern, basic human need, had been overwhelmingly answered. Workers and laborers alike were more than meeting their needs, and the socialists' prime complaint now carried no weight. The line of attack shifted from basic human needs of survival to the more easily corrupted and vulnerable sentiment of human envy. Also, keep in mind that this line of attack could sustain itself in perpetuity, regardless of humanity's increase in prosperity and development as a whole. Even if we could multiply every American's income by a factor of ten without any sort of distorting inflation, inequality would still exist. There is, presumably, no upper limit on the developmental and wealth increases the population makes as a whole. The contention of inequality today will never be satiated by any real positive changes for the population as a whole, and that's simply because it isn't meant to be satiated at all.

While envy is a depressingly effective tool for mobilizing the masses against their perceived oppressors, two major problems with inequality as the new frontier of attack on free market enterprise exist: its implied solution, total equality, is neither possible nor desirable.

Although the basic notion of income equality seems innocent, egalitarian, and desirable enough, it is far too simplistic to encapsulate the infinite complexities that factor into an individual's economic outcomes: personal decisions, work ethic, intelligence, conscientiousness, reliability, raw talent, and countless other relevant factors affect the dollar amount of a final paycheck. A prudent system must reward workers for their meritorious contributions and refuse to artificially equalize incomes as a matter of "fairness." In a free society, individuals will not all make the same decisions, and that is okay. We can't afford to adopt equality as our ultimate measure of desirable incomes because it neutralizes any incentive to create just inequalities through higher effort and better results.

One example above all others solidified this conclusion in my mind forever. Imagine you've enrolled in an organic chemistry class at Harvard University. Assuming the course is four credit hours as is typical, you're paying roughly *six thousand dollars* to take the class. You work your butt off studying late nights and weekends. Through much struggle, time, and effort, you barely scrape an A out of the class, but you don't care how low it is. It's an A, and you earned it. But after all your assignments and exams have been completed, you notice your grade has dropped to a C. Infuriated, you march over to the professor's office to see what happened. After expressing your concern, you receive the following answer:

"You know, it's a real tragedy I had to give you a C, but I'm a big believer in grade equality. In an effort to make the grades more equal, I took points from the high scores and redistributed them to the low scores. Now everyone can at least take home a passing grade. I mean, you wouldn't want the other students to fail, would you? After all, it's not like you know what the struggling students were dealing with this semester. It's not like you earned that grade all on your own."

Don't lie. You wouldn't put up with that, and neither would I. Humans inherently understand we have a right to our own work regardless of the advantages that may have helped us along the way.

Sure, the example is simple, but how far is it really from the sentiments we're already hearing from prominent left-wing voices? Is "You didn't earn this grade" really so different from what Obama told us back in 2012?

"If you've been successful, you didn't get there on your own. You didn't get there on your own. I'm always struck by people who think, 'Well, it must be just because I was just so smart.' There are a lot of smart people out there. 'It must be because I worked harder than everybody else.'… *If you've got a business, you didn't build that. Somebody else made that happen.*"

Of course people help us along the way. No one exists in a complete vacuum devoid of all others. We enter the world naked, helpless, and entirely dependent on goodwill to survive past infancy. Reasonable people know that none of us could survive, let alone thrive, without some external support, but if we can't ultimately be responsible for our own choices and their resultant consequences, can we really be responsible for anything? What about crime? Insults? Can we attribute only our good outcomes to others? Or the bad outcomes as well? Perfect income equality will never be a desirable outcome because it would cost individual agency, personal responsibility, and a complete forfeiture of any pride we could take in our own work or accomplishments because ultimately, it would make no difference.

More importantly, perfect income equality is not possible in one major regard. Any government (especially ours) would be vastly, grossly incapable of effectively implementing actual income equality. But consider also, *how much do you trust the government?* Do you think the bureaucrats in Washington toil away with your best interests at heart? Is it likely that government workers care whether their function serves the interests of the people, "We the People" for whom they supposedly work? Undoubtedly some of them do, I'm sure.

But we would certainly be naive to think that most of them do. They have their own interests.

In a 2018 interview with the Hoover Institution, renowned economist and scholar Thomas Sowell described his experience working with the Department of Labor. Tasked with an assignment of discerning the cause of decreasing jobs in Puerto Rico in the sugar industry, Sowell considered two possibilities, either 1) as economists indicated, folks at the bottom were being priced out of a job, or 2) hurricanes had ravaged Puerto Rico during the sugar harvesting and destroyed the crops, leading to a decreased demand for sugar crop workers. Sowell concluded that in order to discern the causal factor of the job decrease, he needed to find out how much sugar crop was standing in the fields *before* the hurricane struck. Upon revealing the need for this crucial data to his colleagues and superiors at the Department of Labor, he was met with pushback, cumbersome red tape, and pessimism. Told he would have to submit a request to the secretary of labor for the information, he did just that. He is still awaiting a response.

> *The U.S. Department of Labor administers the minimum wage law, and the money and careers of perhaps a third or some other significant percentage of the Labor Department's other resources come from administering the minimum wage law...the government is not out there at the personification of the national interest. They have their own interests, and the Labor Department's was clearly an interest in keeping the minimum wage.*

It's not about your interests. It's about the interest of the government. Government could never provide income equality. If the government can't even provide equality under the law, and someone like Jussie Smollett can buy his way out of criminal charges (roughly, the case has gotten more complicated since he was initially charged), why should we believe that the government could provide income equality? We all agree that equality under the law is a good and necessary mandate. As my good friend Joe Biden once tweeted, "No one is above the law—not even the president," but anyone with their eyes open can clearly see the government is incapable of delivering the mandate we all agree on: equality under the law. Brock Turner served three months in prison for a rape he did commit. Brian Banks spent almost six years in prison for a rape he did not commit. Kristian Saucier took six photos in classified areas on his personal cell phone and was sentenced to a full year in prison. Hillary Clinton emailed classified material from a private account and—ha, who am I kidding? You already know she'll never spend a day behind bars. I could go on forever, but you get the point.

It would be unwise to believe that a government incapable of providing equality under the law could ever create "income equality," and even if it could, we often carry to the economy the same sense of fairness we held in the classroom: we deserve to keep what we earn. Our ability to do so affirms the value of our work. What we need are fair rules by which we function within an economy, the resultant disparities be damned.

Cronyism: God Bless the Rich

When I was seven years old, my older brother rubbed his dirty, stinky socks in my face, much to my peril. Being the ruthless seven-year-old that I was, I spat back, "I hate you!" Each of us ran downstairs to tattle on the other, submitting our grievances to our dad in hopes of the other's demise.

"All right, I'll be upstairs soon to dish out the spankings," he said. Notice that word is plural. "Spankings" with an *s* at the end…as in, more than one. Anyhoo, I went to bed that night with a sore bottom (which I deserved) and a bitter attitude that my big brother had gotten away with his dirty laundry assault.

Growing up, I needed a good swat more than once to put me in my place and check my remarkably stubborn attitude, but that is the only one I vividly remember. Not because it was excessively painful or because it was particularly unjust, but because I felt the disciplinary rules had been unfairly applied to me but not to my likewise guilty brother—and that stuck.

In a much more serious and consequential reality, I believe the American people have awakened to the fact that little people are not playing under the same economic rules as big corporations and wealthy elites. In the 2020 Democratic debates, Senator Sanders remarked:

> *What are we talking about? We are living in many ways in a socialist society right now. The problem is, as Dr. Martin Luther King reminded us, we have socialism for the very rich and rugged individualism for the very poor.*

For once, I agree with Bernie Sanders. Although Americans have implemented a comparatively moderate but growing welfare state for the poor, it pales in comparison to the excessive and reckless bailouts of dishonest, mismanaged, or otherwise failing corporations. Special economic privileges for ultra-rich folks run antithetical to the spirit of free market enterprise. It's not the government's job to pick the winners and losers of the economy, but that's just what they often do. It's cronyism, plain and simple.

When well-connected, ultra-wealthy corporations lobby heavily for legislation that supports their commercial interests—at the expense of the taxpayer—they are seeking a form of socialist aid. This is not free market enterprise, it's naked corruption and government favoritism. Cronyism comes in many forms: biased laws intended to rig the scales in favor of certain financial interests, unearned tax breaks, artificially high prices—much of this at the cost of the general public. Whether that ultimate cost is a billion-dollar bailout, artificially high prices on certain goods, or billions in tax forgiveness, you can be certain the proletariat will cover that cost to the pleasure of the bourgeoisie.

It's not hard to understand. The cause is sadly predictable: money. Big corporations have long used the underhand practice of offering legislators lucrative jobs on boards and committees for which they have no relevant experience following their term in office, and too often, it gets them what they want, whatever that might be. This is beyond wrong.

If Americans want to preserve our free, capitalist economy, our leaders have to be willing to legislate on behalf of our interests, and their record shows quite clearly that they do not. They legislate on behalf of their personal interests.

Understand me clearly: this is not to say that all government subsidies are inherently bad. Certain subsidies help ensure the continuation of vital sectors of the economy that might otherwise be left unable to compete on the global market. Sectors like agriculture, for example, might pose a significant security threat to the greater population if completely outsourced. A hypothetical war with, say, China, could quickly produce an utter crisis should we find ourselves mostly dependent on their agricultural imports for food. It's easy to see how external dependence on critical commodities could quickly devolve into a national security nightmare. However, it seems pretty clear that the vast majority of such one-sided legislation cannot be viewed through any possible lens of "national security," and when this happens, we should push back.

Cronyism is not just contrary to free markets, it's a threat to democracy. In professor Robert Reich's *Saving Capitalism*, he traces the issues of manipulated patent laws, biased legislation, and crooked policy-making used to line the pockets of the rich and the powerful. One thing is certain, if Republicans denounced every whiff of cronyism the way they do every trace of socialism, America might not have this problem. But alas, we do.

CHAPTER 7

BORIS YELTSIN'S INFATUATION

When I saw those shelves crammed with hundreds, thousands of cans, cartons, and goods of every possible sort, for the first time I felt quite frankly sick with despair for the Soviet people. That such a potentially super-rich country as ours has been brought to a state of such poverty! It is terrible to think of it.

—Boris Yeltsin, *Against the Grain*

URING THE EARLY DAYS OF the COVID-19 pandemic, when saying things like "fifteen days to slow the spread" was still fashionable, people panicked in very real, tangible ways. Most notably, countless grocery stores across the country looked like they had been ransacked. Empty shelves and barren aisles... People. Freaked. Out. Countless Twitter us-ers took the startling anomaly as evidence of capitalism's failure. Even Pope Francis declared it had failed us in the pandemic.

"This is what capitalism looks like during a time of crisis!" cried some of the scared voices, seemingly unaware of the basic mechanics of supply and demand. Others like Ben Shapiro quickly noted the apparently little-known reality that barren shelves and foodless supermarkets are painfully commonplace in socialist countries. Free market enterprise had stocked the shelves in the first place, and that very same system refilled the shelves shortly after they were emptied.

I'll be the first to admit the empty shelves were scary. What were we supposed to do when we finished off the food in our pantries and fridges? However, *we have to step back and take a look at the consistent norms of our lives under capitalism rather than the unfortunate crises that may temporarily disrupt them.*

Empty grocery stores have long been a hallmark of fully implemented socialism. No one was more keenly aware of the barrenness and hunger the Russian people endured under such scarcity than Boris Yeltsin, a Communist Party member who became the first president of Russia during the dissolution of the U.S.S.R. in 1991. The Soviet Union's collectivized economy had been underproducing for his entire life.

During Yeltsin's visit to the United States in 1989, he toured our most eminent sites: the Trump Tower amid skyscrapers in New York City, the NASA Center, and other notable landmarks. But what really caught his attention was a Randall's grocery store in Clear Lake, Texas. Yes, seriously. During his American tour, he unexpectedly requested a trip to a grocery store. He wanted to see what life was like for the everyday American. It proved one of the most transformative experiences of his political life. Some believe it prompted his 180-degree turn against communism in favor of capitalism.

Yeltsin could not believe the abundant bounty of frozen, dried, packaged, canned, and fresh goods before his eyes. He was even more surprised to discover the store opened for all people, regardless of political party or class affiliation. "Even the Politburo [Soviet political elite] do not have access to luxury foods such as these."

The sheer amount of choices in the store deeply impressed him. He was especially enamored of some type of frozen chocolate pudding pop, weirdly enough. The experience cut his heart deeply. He now knew what his people back home were missing out on. In the biography written by his close assistant, the author noted the despair and visible sorrow Yeltsin experienced on his plane rides across America and back to Russia. The crushing scarcity his own countrymen lived under ate away at his mind and heart. He solemnly noted, "If the Russian countrymen were to see this, there would be a revolution." Although Yeltsin was largely unsuccessful at implementing free market reforms in his homeland, the experience left him forever changed.

When we talk of the failures of free market enterprise, or capitalism, we often neglect to incorporate one critical and perhaps even counterintuitive question: *Failures as compared to what?*" For Americans like me who were born and raised in an economy of prosperity, it can be difficult to see the leaps and bounds that free market enterprise has made for our quality of life. It's difficult to identify what we've been surrounded by our entire lives. We can always find the bad. We're hardwired to see the negative wherever we go. The luxury and wealth so common to Americans are easily taken for granted as the unchangeable and enduring reality that cannot be lost.

But it can.

How do we make the economy work for everyone? How do we help the poor? We embrace free market enterprise. The more history I learn and the more knowledge I gain, the more gratitude I feel for this system that has brought us unbelievable prosperity. Real privilege is living under capitalism. We don't recognize such luxury because it has become the background expectations of life as we know it. Electricity? Virtually 100 percent of Americans have it—and have since 1990. Air conditioning? About 90 percent of us have it. Running water and indoor plumbing? Nearly all of us have it.

In this chapter, I want to share with you the two most convincing truths that finally pulled me out of my leftist, socialist fog. First, the undeniable historical progress made under free markets. Second, the fact that such free markets fuel the Nordic countries as well, despite their reputation as the collective poster child of socialism.

Leaps and Bounds

Mercer University has a mantra plastered on every sign, hat, and free T-shirt it gives away. "At Mercer, everyone majors in changing the world." I always used to find the mantra pleasant, if cheesy, and my dad would scoff, "Yeah, right. Everyone majors in finding a job."

But one economics professor changed my perspective forever. On the first day of class, he mentioned the school's well-known mantra. Then he said something I never expected to hear from a professor.

"Don't tell the administrators I said this, but I totally disagree. I actually think the world is a really good place. I don't want to change it. It's already gotten much, much better." He then proceeded to prove to the class exactly what I hope to prove to you.

Free market enterprise has dramatically improved the quality *and* quantity of life for *billions* of people around the world. Let me prove it to you.

Wherever capitalism is adopted, people become richer, healthier, live longer, and enjoy higher overall standards of living. In the last fifty years alone, capitalism has enabled two *billion* people to lift themselves out of poverty, as noted by Harvard economist Arthur Brooks. Up until this life-changing class, I never knew any of this. I never knew that life was improving for vast numbers of the poorest people around the world. I didn't believe it, and chances are, you might not either. Please, let me prove you wrong the way my professor proved me wrong. I bet you'll be encouraged to hear what massive strides humanity has made as it has embraced free market enterprise. I know I sure was.

First, many intellectuals become weary of the discussion of progress because they are rightly concerned about the uneven distribution of said progress. This is a legitimate concern, which I would like to address as best I can. We must first acknowledge it is impossible to disseminate that which does not exist.

Capitalism best allows for new technologies to cross from the realm of abstract cognition to the functioning iPhone in your back pocket. We may vilify the profit incentive, but it's wildly effective in getting critical technology to the masses. Additionally, no technological, agricultural, or otherwise useful innovation during the course of human history was immediately accessible to all upon its arrival on the market. Innovation takes specialization, refining, and improvement for its price to fall to a level accessible to the masses. While we should continue to strive for accessibility for all, we must do so with a clear-headed conception of how to get there.

Second, the vast majority of the material improvement of the human condition has occurred within the last two hundred years. From astronomical medical improvements to plummeting death rates to increased availability of the basic resources needed to survive, humanity has made more progress in the last two centuries than in the previous eighteen centuries combined. Make no mistake, the people born in the last two hundred years don't happen to be the select geniuses of history, despite the Flynn effect demonstrating that global IQ is increasing on a yearly basis thanks to better nutrition. Rather, societies have adopted new, inclusive economic systems—namely, free market enterprise—that have enabled humanity to tap into the intellect and ingenuity of the masses rather than the few. This is what's responsible for the massive leap forward we're enjoying today... whether we realize it or not.

Let's go through three of free market enterprise's greatest achievements.

Lifespan Doubled

Life expectancy stands as one of the most salient unnoticeable realities.

For the vast, vast majority of human history, humans could expect less than half the lifespan many of us enjoy today. This reality is true not only for modern industrialized nations, but for all nations as the advancements of modern medicine and the products of capitalism have us living longer, healthier lives.

In the last two hundred years, the adoption of free markets as a result of the Enlightenment has produced explosive improvements never before seen in the course of human history. No one thinks twice about the existence of nursing homes or the reality that most people know their grandparents. Capitalism not only has effectively doubled our lifespan across the board but also granted us the opportunity to know more about our ancestors than was previously possible.

As noted by Ronald Bailey and Marian Tupy of the Cato Institute in their recently released book, *Ten Global Trends Every Smart Person Should Know*, at one point,

> *Average life expectancy at birth for people hovered at about 30 years for most of human history…about one-third of children died before they reached their fifth birthday. Only 4 percent of the world's population generally lived to be older than 65 years of age before the 20th century.*

But the spread of free market enterprise and rapid development would soon change that. "During the past 200 years, global life expectancy has more than doubled, now reaching more than 72 years according to the World Bank." We cannot afford to overlook this monumental progress.

A massive contributor to this radical upward trend hits home for mothers: infant mortality and death of children before the age of five years. You're a good person; you don't want children to needlessly die. This system has best allowed for children to prosper and live past their first few hours in the world and beyond their fifth birthdays. Bailey and Tupy again succinctly make the case. "The world population grew from 1.6 billion in 1900 to 7.7 billion in 2019 not because people are breeding like rabbits, but because they are no longer dropping like flies.... Until the 19th century, nearly 60 percent of children died from disease, starvation, or violence before reaching adulthood." A system that produces results such as these must be carefully weighed even in light of its flaws. Our lifespans are tangible and tied to the economic systems that sustain them.

Quality of Life Skyrockets

Free market enterprise has risen to the challenge of providing for the masses. Sorry, Karl.

While such economically free societies show no absolute trend in type of government, they do show consistent trends in capacity for opportunity. Heck, capitalism is so damningly effective in improving the economy and well-being of a population that even the Chinese Communist Party has figured out a way to harness its immeasurable capacity to produce wealth and progress through "free market zones." Smart political "communists" implement capitalism because *they know it works.*

Again, the reality of our wealth comes not in the shiny or flashy things but in the everyday realities that we come to take for granted. Throughout the course of humanity, most humans have not even owned a bed. But I bet you do. Throughout the course of history, most humans have not been able to read. But you can. Throughout history, the vast majority of humans have never had the opportunity to watch a movie on a screen or make a telephone call. I'd bet my life you've probably done both. By all historical standards, we are rich.

Do not misunderstand me: I'm not saying every person who lives in a capitalist economy has an easy life, but it would be ludicrous to disregard the undeniable progress this system has provided us. We're living better and longer than we ever have. Let's stop and smell the roses, because we surely have the time to now. While we must continue to strive for progress, we must also look back to see how we've gotten this far.

Again, I'm not saying shut up and be grateful. I'm saying let's pause and tread cautiously so as not to sink the ship that has brought us from the previously inconceivable brutality of disease, death, and poverty to the massively prosperous current state of wealth, health, and plenty. Consider the following facts:

- Famine, a massive cause of death historically, has been virtually eradicated from every corner of the globe except for those that fall under war zones.

- Our ability to safeguard ourselves from natural-disaster deaths has exponentially increased. Bailey and Tupy note, "The chance of dying from a natural catastrophe—earthquake, flood, drought, storm, wildfire, landslide, or epidemic—has declined by 99% since the 1920s and 1930s."

- "Nearly 90% of the world's population in 1820 was illiterate. Today almost 90% can read." Congratulations to you on joining the majority.

These powerful data points represent a small fraction of the massive leaps forward for humanity. Such trends include the reduction of racist attitudes; the reduction of air pollution; reduced violent crime; improved access to clean drinking water, technology, electricity, and more; and the expansion of affordable housing. If these data points intrigue you, I highly recommend you read *Ten Global Trends Every Smart Person Should Know*. The title may be cheesy, but the content is encouraging, fascinating, and most importantly, based in fact.

Poverty Antidote

Wealth best combats poverty, and free market enterprise best produces wealth. At the end of the day, most of us across the political spectrum want the same things: a chance to put food on the table, affordable housing, a decent standard of living, and the belief that the opportunities and resources we leave our kids will be greater than the ones we got. Free market enterprise has paved the way for this reality. In the last fifty years alone, it has enabled *two billion* people to lift themselves out of poverty, most of them in China and India.

If we want to continue the upward trend for countless aspects of our lives, we must protect this system which has produced far beyond what anyone could have imagined in centuries past. Researchers estimate that in 1820, almost 85 percent of the world's population was living on less than $1.90 per person per day. As of 2018, the World Bank estimated that only 8.6 percent of the world's population lived in such extreme poverty. It doesn't stop there. "In 1800, average global income stood at roughly $1,140 per person per year. By 2016, income had risen to $14,574 per person per year" Tupy cites from economic historian Angus Maddison at the University of Groningen. This statistic is adjusted for purchasing power parity. It represents real change. That means average global income has increased by a multiple of nearly thirteen over the past two hundred years.

If you hate poverty, free market enterprise is your best friend. No other system on earth—not charity, not government aid, and certainly not socialism—has enabled billions to lift themselves out of poverty like it has. Those who frame capitalism as exploitative mistakenly overlook the unprecedented and almost unbelievable wealth capitalism has put into the hands of poor people around the globe.

Don't Buy the Nordic Lie

Supporters and leaders on the political left constantly point to Denmark and other Nordic countries as their model for America. *Scandinavian socialism is the best socialism,* they assert with passion. "I think we should look to countries like Denmark, like Sweden, and Norway and learn from what they have accomplished for their working people," Bernie Sanders argued back on October 15, 2015. The trend seems pretty consistent with just about any left-leaning person I've spoken with. They're constantly enthralled by the high standards of living and overall prosperity the Nordic countries enjoy. They want that here in the United States. What's so bad about that? Don't we want the U.S. to succeed? Why not emulate the Nordic countries?

Minimal scrutiny of such a prescription for America quickly renders such an argument ludicrous. Let me give you eight reasons why.

- They've got their terminology entirely wrong.
- Their economic system is not socialism; it's largely capitalism.
- Cultural aspects of the Nordic countries uniquely prepare them for their exceptionally large welfare state.
- These countries have extremely small populations compared to the U.S.
- Virtually all of their military expenses have been outsourced to the United States.
- Racial and ethnic homogeneity play a massive role in their success and cohesion. They hold a deeply ethno-national identity nonexistent in the U.S.
- Strong community bonds disincentivize abuse of government services.
- They're moving away from this unsustainable model.

First, the far-left progressives will point to the Nordic countries as their model for democratic socialism in America, but
they fail to realize this isn't even the term the Nordic countries
use to describe themselves! As I mentioned in an earlier chapter,
the term "socialism" has come to mean everything and nothing
at all. The broad array of economic systems who reasonably
lay claim to the term has fostered division and confusion, but
the Nordic countries view themselves as forms of "social democracy," not some type of socialism. To characterize them as
socialist is not only contrary to the nature of their systems, it is
contrary to the way they identify themselves.

Second, their economic system is *not* socialism. It's free
market capitalism, but don't take my word for it. The tendency
of the American left to characterize Scandinavia as socialist grew
to such prominence that the prime minister of Denmark had
to publicly refute it. At the John F. Kennedy Jr. Forum in 2015,
Lars Rasmussen stated,

> *I know that people in the U.S. associate the Nordic
> model with some sort of socialism. Therefore, I
> would like to make one thing clear: Denmark is
> far from a socialist planned economy. Denmark
> is a market economy. The Nordic model is an
> expanded welfare state which provides a high level
> of security for its citizens, but it is also a successful
> market economy, with much freedom to pursue
> your dreams and live your life as you wish.*

Now, you may rightly point out my contradiction here. I
previously stated that control of greater amounts of money is a

form of socialism. This is a bit tricky because it is difficult to separate money as a resource. Paying taxes doesn't mean you live under socialism. That should be obvious. I think the water gets murky when high, progressive tax rates border punitive or confiscatory levels. It's difficult to say precisely what those would be, but the Nordic countries would certainly be in the running. The highly progressive tax rate, as you may recall, was also one of Marx's ideal outcomes. While many aspects of the Nordic countries can be easily explained, I do struggle with this fully free market label for populations paying often half or more of their income in taxes.

Third, most of the Nordic countries have cultural factors that foster not only their high social trust but also uniquely equip them for the type of economic system they've adopted. The Nordic countries, while largely secular, retained their Protestant work ethic and strongly believe in the value of cooperation and giving back. Their high social cohesion and cultural homogeneity make their population perfectly equipped for functioning well within the system. It's a vastly different demographic and cultural reality than we have in America.

Fourth, in terms of population, the Nordic countries individually boast populations akin to small American states. Sweden has almost eleven million people. Denmark has almost six million. Finland has roughly five and a half million people. Switzerland has slightly over eight and a half million. You get the point. So on the higher end of the population spectrum, we're talking about countries roughly the size of Ohio. Does it make any logical sense to take a system that works for a tiny state and transfer it to the nearly 330 million people living in the United

States? Of course not. Besides the fact that a majority of voters in the U.S. have so far shown by their votes they do not want this system, American emphasis on freedom of all kinds makes this option unappealing in many regards.

Fifth, in their strong alliance with the U.S., the Nordic countries have largely outsourced their military expenditures to the United States, which spent roughly a staggering $630 billion on defense in 2020 alone. In contrast, Sweden spent a mere $6.6 billion on its military in 2019, Denmark a mere $4 billion, Finland $3.85 billion in 2017, and so on. Is there any question whether these countries would up their spending if not aligned with the most highly funded and most powerful military on the face of the planet? This intelligent outsourcing of basic needs, like security, to the United States frees up Nordic tax dollars for social welfare programs such as those they currently sustain.

Sixth, the Nordic countries have one trait conducive to their social cohesion and high levels of social trust. It is a trait the U.S. will (I pray) never have: an ethno-national identity. Some Nordic countries, like Denmark, pride themselves not only on the systems they have created, but also the ethnic bloodlines from which they have descended. This racial and cultural homogeneity is, in part, responsible for the wild success the Nordic countries have experienced. Nima Sanandaji, an Iranian Swede himself, notes the massive impact of homogeneity on outcomes for various countries. He notes that the top six most equal countries in the world, in terms of wealth, are neither mostly capitalist nor mostly socialist, but they are all largely homogeneous. While this does not prove causation, it points heavily to the idea that perhaps racial and cultural sameness plays a part in the equalizing of wealth outcomes.

Seventh, these populations face massive disincentives to abuse social programs. This social check on the population has helped maintain what viability still exists for the Nordic welfare states. Swedes feel a greater connection to each other and thus a responsibility not to misuse public services. On the other hand, the likelihood that a wealthy cosmopolitan in San Francisco feels any social, emotional, or obligatory tie to a corn farmer in Iowa as a matter of logic is extremely low. They share little cultural, socioeconomic, or political overlap with one another. When you boil it down, they live in completely different worlds. Urban versus rural. Democrat versus Republican. Elite versus common. White collar versus blue collar. And so on. America's large size and widely different states make quite obvious the possibility for a similar connectedness and social trust is zero.

Finally, especially as seen with Sweden, the Nordic countries currently face long-term issues of viability. As their population ages, the workforce has shrunk. The system as it stands requires massive reform to fund itself. Options to maintain the viability of these programs would dismay any reasonable person. They're looking at raising taxes on the already most highly taxed populations in the world. The Danes, for example, pay anywhere in the ballpark of 56 percent to 74 percent of their income in taxes. Can you imagine making $100,000 in a given year and only taking home twenty-six grand? Geez, that's depressing.

I could go on about how their policies don't even reflect those the democratic socialists want for America. Most Nordic countries have no minimum wage. Most also maintain strict immigration policies, but the democratic socialists in America are calling for the opposite. However, I think you get the idea. We're not like Scandinavia, and we can't realistically expect to stamp their economic policies on our vastly different, larger, more diverse nation.

Takeaway

They say you never know what you've got till it's gone, but I say you never know what you've got till you realize the vast majority of humans throughout history lived without most of the things you enjoy every day.

When we talk about human progress, we think of skyscrapers, airplanes, rockets, and computers. What we fail to realize is that the greatest progress ever made has been the rapid enhancement of every aspect of our lives under the most inclusive economic system: free market enterprise. Over the last two hundred years, it has led to less poverty, higher literacy rates, better health care, more technology, safer homes and buildings, and more political representation.

As if the accomplishments of capitalism weren't enough, socialists cannot point to a single pure socialist success story—present or past—because there is not one. From the U.S.S.R. to Venezuela to countless other nations, socialism has produced nothing but poverty, destruction, and death. Those who would point to the Nordic countries as their example of socialist success only deceive themselves. Scandinavia better protects free markets than the United States even if their tax rates are startling. Don't let them fool you. A welfare state is a question of government policy up for debate, but we can't even begin that debate without the free market enterprise economy to pay for it in the first place.

Free market enterprise, like any other human idea, is not perfect, but it has produced a standard of living high enough to convert the most powerful socialists on earth to free market lovers. By all measures, this system has given us a standard of living never previously thought possible. It has given us prosperity beyond Boris Yeltsin's wildest dreams.

CHAPTER 8

DOG-FACED PONY
SOLDIER, OVER
AND OUT!

I HAVE TO BE HONEST, AS I near the conclusion of this book, my first instinct is to raise my hands and lay some Nietzsche on you, to leave you with the same statement he so casually dropped in his preface: "If this book is unintelligible to anyone and hard on the ears, the fault, as I see it, does not necessarily lie with me," but I will do my best not to fall into such temptation.

When Joe Biden insulted me, he inadvertently changed the entire trajectory of my life, but in a strange way, I harbor a small hope he might have changed the trajectory of this country. His old age and cognitive decline have led him to unwittingly speak the quiet parts out loud. If the disdain he feels for normal people wasn't clear in what he said to me, it certainly became clearer when later that year he told an industrial worker he was "full of s---," when he told black people they "ain't black" if they don't vote for him, and when video footage surfaced of him calling American veterans "stupid b------s" to their faces.

This point is much bigger than anything to do with Biden, and for all I know, he could very well be president by the time this book is published. His campaign presents an invaluable warning to the American people because of what it has so transparently demonstrated: Biden and the political elites like him disdain normal people like you...like me. At the deepest core of socialism, I believe, is that same disdain for the common man, for his ability to make his way in life on his own merits. *You can't do it, so we, the enlightened few, will do it for you.*

Academics, politicians, and "the robes" (judges, lawyers, and professors) at large haven't told young people the whole story. We're taught the shortcomings of the free market system without the context of the undeniable, explosive humanitarian progress it has yielded, affecting every aspect of our lives. These half-truths permeate our curriculum, our popular culture, and ultimately, our minds.

A 2018 Gallup poll found that of Americans aged eighteen to twenty-nine, just over half felt positively about socialism (51 percent) while less than half felt positively toward capitalism (45 percent). Frank Newport noted in Gallup News, "This represents a 12-point decline in young adults' positive views of capitalism in just the past two years." More than this, it's a majority-changing shift within the last decade from the 68 percent who viewed capitalism positively in 2010. Young

Americans' perspective of a fair economic system no longer includes free market enterprise as we know it.

I wrote this book because I once bought those lies too. Heck, I nearly got frostbite knocking on doors for Andrew Yang during the February primary (a slight exaggeration, but you get the idea). Unlearning such lies gave me hope, encouragement, and a substantiated belief that the future can be better than the past, but that will depend on us. Such news of incredible progress has been wrongfully denied to me and my peers, and it's time for that to change. But it won't make any difference unless we work to preserve the system of prosperity we've inherited. Fear of the future has wrongfully driven us to call for a system that has bred nothing but destruction, tyranny, poverty, and death. We're told this time it will be "different." It will be "democratic." But history indicates otherwise. As we rise to meet the challenges of our time, I hope we can do so with a clear understanding of the giant shoulders we're standing on and a cautious respect and gratitude for what we've been given.

Don't Let It End Here

Hard times create strong men. Strong men create good times. Good times create weak men. And, weak men create hard times.
　　　　—G. Michael Hopf, *Those Who Remain*

We've got a lot to lose. I can't be sure of the expiration date, but I feel quite certain freedom can't continue without our rising to be worthy of it. Perhaps our complacency in plenty has eroded our ability or desire to preserve our inheritance. Whatever the case, I feel quite strongly there may be hard times ahead. They have certainly been an option on our ballots. More than this, such destruction is not only possible, it's fast. Slow, steady progress is not news, only our destruction of it. Johan Galtung and Mari Holmboe Ruge made this reality clear in the *Journal of Peace Research.*

> *There is a basic asymmetry in life between the positive, which is difficult and takes time, and the negative, which is much easier and takes less time—compare the amount of time needed to bring up and socialize an adult person and the amount of time needed to kill him in an accident, the amount of time needed to build a house and to destroy it in a fire, to make an airplane and to crash it, and so on.*

Let's be honest, we're at serious risk of crashing the plane.

As reported by *The Hill,* seven in ten millennials say they would vote for a socialist; in fact, some aren't even saving for retirement because they don't believe capitalism will exist by the time they get to retirement age. Whatever your views on economics, I humbly advise you...do not do *that.* Young people eagerly expect massive changes to our economy as we know it, and anyone who says we aren't at risk of losing our economic freedoms is either not paying attention or lying. President Ronald Reagan rightly warned us that freedom is never more than a generation away from extinction, and this generation seems to no longer even want it. I fear we just might be that weak link in the chain, and should that prove to be the case, there truly are dark times ahead.

Overwhelming historical evidence, scientific data, and moral philosophy point to one conclusion: socialism destroys human prosperity, and free market enterprise fosters it. The growing admiration for the downright dangerous ideology of socialism is no accident. Khrushchev may have been right after all. Maybe he didn't need bullets to fight us. There can be no doubt: we are self-destructing. The challenges we face are real, but the far-left solutions we champion to solve them can only lead to greater disaster. It's precisely what has happened in the past. Socialism, rather than ushering in an egalitarian utopia, cost tens of millions of lives over the course of the twentieth century, destroying civil rights and liberties along the way. Such precedent cannot be taken lightly. I fear we may be the generation to fulfill the predictions of a "somewhat obscure Scotsman" from the eighteenth century echoed in the *Daily Oklahoman* in 1951.

A democracy cannot exist as a permanent form of government. It can only exist until a majority discovers it can vote itself largess [a generous amount of money] out of the public treasury. After that, the majority always votes for the candidate promising the most benefits with the result the democracy collapses because of the loose fiscal policy ensuing, always to be followed by a dictatorship, then a monarchy.

I pray he is wrong, but I fear he is right.

APPENDIX:
A BONUS INTERVIEW

Few people can cut through culture and politics to understand deeper, broader implications. This man can. Under the
condition of anonymity, he agreed to be interviewed for this
book. He is the very same anonymous professor cited in the
Acknowledgments, and his input has been invaluable to the
creation of this book.

How would you characterize the push for socialism today?

Examples exist for almost any explanation. What is new and
unprecedented is a particular kind of mix. Never has society
had a population as literate as ours. We are approaching 100
percent literacy. But when uneducated literate people can engage
the political process, the game is changed. Those who think of
things beyond their immediate surroundings. The bottom level
of education has a lot of power for the first time in human history. They have an equal vote. Additionally, there is a constant
barrage of misinformation from news; this allows the elite to
control everyone all the time through use of the media. It used
to take three weeks to get news from Boston to London. Now

the U.S. left, since it controls all news everywhere, can pull off COVID restrictions, which tank the economy in an election year. It sets the stage for power consolidation from beyond the nation state.

We are witnessing power consolidation—the victory of leftist ideologues. They have already won. Trump is slowing the inevitable. He is simply slowing the avalanche.

Who made the decisions for the COVID restrictions? Never before in history have we quarantined the healthy. I gauge the morality of the society on how it treats the least powerful. The elderly are vulnerable, but what we did had nothing to do with saving them and everything to do with hurting the economy. It wasn't a conspiracy. Everybody realized the opportunity, and the right didn't have the political will to stand up to it.

Can we stop it?

I have faith in the American people believing that individual liberty matters. You can sway minds on this. Things could get so bad. The fact that President Trump is President Trump is a profound sign that there is a silent America. I wouldn't say this to my neighbors, but I am going to support Trump. I also believe there is much wishful thinking and lying in the exit polls. It is nobody's damn business who I voted for. We elected a rightist. Hillary is not a buffoon; she's super well-connected. The American people could wake up.

What do you think socialism has to offer Americans or humanity?

Nothing whatsoever. Not as a way of thinking, living, or acting. It is organic collectivism: helping homeless folks, helping battered women, helping the disenfranchised.

I do believe in people doing good outside of government, doing good in local governance. Principles of social justice can make profound change at the local government. True leaders will graduate and leave. Local governance works very similarly. Voluntary collectivist action takes place locally. Federal government exists only to protect us from everything else.

Socialist principles are utopian and not good. Social justice principles should exist on a voluntary basis.

What do you think is the greatest danger that socialism poses to Americans?

I don't think socialism holds any power at all, but socialists pose an extreme danger to the American way of life, liberty, and security. It might be less clear that they endanger physical security. The same people that don't want Americans to have guns do not want police either. You take away guns and then you take the police away, you now have Hobbesian anarchy.

We must maintain law and order to preserve life. In Wisconsin, people leave once they get an education. People don't leave Philadelphia. You vote with your feet; you change the government or you move. For some, it is inconceivable to move for political reasons.

France has race riots because they made it incredibly attractive to Middle Easterners. Same with Democrats and Texas. Coasts are so "left" relative to the center of the country (socialists are having more success on the coasts). As a historian, the results of this are that the local government makes things better for everyone, but also the leftists who wanted to live there.

We've had socialized health care since the '70s. Medicare and Medicaid grossly inflate the value of health care.

What do you believe has produced the recent surge in demand for socialism in America? Could it in part be due to a decades-long American academic climate of shunning Marxism out of respect for the sacrosanct cow of capitalism?

I think it is due to a conscious infiltration of education at all levels. Communism was very popular in the '20s and '30s in America. Socialism tried and failed in the political marketplace; they chose to infiltrate the public school system. During the Cold War, they had to keep their heads down. They have been teaching socialism since the late '80s on purpose. The education system has been infiltrated purposefully.

The Nazi final solution was not a conscious decision. Individuals helped further the goal of Nazi leadership with legitimate decisions, just like those on the left are trying to socialize the American public. More socialists make it more acceptable. In the '90s, all the leftist historians would say it was the Russians who ruined the experiment: so, so, so bad. Russians suck, and that is why the experiment failed. The reason Marxism failed in Russia was because of the Russians, they said. That comes from these scholars writing that communism failed because of the Russians. Administrators might not have realized this. But faculty know.

So you're saying they don't want democratic socialism, they want power.

It's a jealous argument. More millionaires mean more middle class. The government is incapable of creating wealth; the government eats wealth. They produce nothing. But if a rich person has that money, they create wealth. The economy is not finite.

Thank you so much for your time. Give me some "takeaways" from your research and experience.

Political ideas exist on a circular spectrum. The far left and the far right begin to overlap as you go further and further out from the center. They begin to use the same tactics to enforce their political ideas and tyrannical measures to secure their own power. For example, excluding certain voices based on inalienable traits (race, sex, religion, etc.) is an explicitly fascist technique. It effectively silences those who would disagree by cutting them off from the dialogue in an irrevocable fashion.

The rank-and-file adherents to an ideology actually believe in the ideology. They chant the slogans, they buy the essential cause behind the movement. However, the higher you go up the ranks, the less and less the adherents believe in the movement and the more the adherents care about simply securing power for their party rather than promulgating the causes of the movement. This was demonstrated by the interviews of the Nazis at the Nuremberg trials and was well documented by Hannah Arendt in her writings.

Socialism is an ideology. Capitalism is not. An ideology consists of an encompassing worldview and a political agenda to implement the purported aims that best confront that worldview. It is explicitly designed to engage political processes to secure power and implement its own society on others. An ideology has a worldview; it is based in a broader political and philosophical movement. Capitalism, however, is not an ideology. It is a mere description of how free markets work when given the space to do so. It does not require greater power on behalf of the government, but rather less. It is a call for less government intervention rather than more. In a certain way, capitalism is an anti-ideology because it allows for more or less any form of worldview so long as it abides by the non-harm and nonaggression principles.

Socialism existed before Karl Marx. He did not, in fact, create socialism, which existed long before he did.

Socialism, more than any other thing, is about securing power over people. It is not about helping the poor. It is not about equality. It is about power. It is important for you to know that the socialists have already won. Trump is simply delaying the inevitable.

Never before have we seen a society as literate as ours. We are approaching 100 percent literacy in the population, and when everyone has a vote, the powerful are highly incentivized to sway the opinions of the masses through their deliberate manipulation via their control of the media. The masses are prey to the powerful who would seek to exploit the democratic process by unfairly influencing the many to do their bidding.

Additionally, given the technological globalization of our age, we must recognize the capacity for bigger and scarier actors to manipulate the masses and consolidate power on a global scale. We must recognize that there is now, more than ever, potential for political consolidation on a global stage, likely under the guise of socialism.

The hoi polloi have come to recognize their own ability to exploit the political process and vote in benefits for themselves. There used to be more shame about this sort of incentive, but now it is overt and lauded with the sanctification of the victim. We are victims and consequently we deserve goodies.

Another critical component to recognize in socialism is Marx's intent that not only are the bourgeois to be overthrown but that the proletariat are incapable of ruling over themselves. The masses can never be trusted with their own governance, but rather a small sect of the bourgeois will rise to power again to rule over the masses in an egalitarian fashion. You must recognize here: all the philosophy is undergirded by a deep condescension and disdain for working-class people. They are incapable of patriotism, family unity, or self-rule. They are incompetent monkeys who do not know what is good for them. We know what is good for them, and consequently, we need the power to dictate our conceptions of what is good for the proletariat.

Elite socialists from China and from Russia have infiltrated our school systems to make us hate America and love socialism.

It is overtly apparent with the current generation, but the goal of it is to make us hate our own country and destroy it from within. If you don't recognize your country as something good or worth saving, why would you preserve it?

Another important factor in socialism is the silencing of dissent. If truth does not matter, whoever has the gun determines truth. Power determines truth. This is not the world we want to live in, but we are already witnessing it before our very eyes. The fascist technique I mentioned above of silencing dissent based on unchangeable God-given characteristics helps facilitate this effective silencing.

Another component of the doctrine of socialist approval is the inherently racist denouncement of the Russians as a terrible society and people incapable of "properly implementing the perfect form of socialism." What you have to understand is that every form of actual socialism has failed. Every single one in history ever. That is reality. You cannot run from it or change it.

Another thing we must be wary of in the way of socialism is the use of identity politics to enforce the ideology on everyone else. There is a systematic bullying which is playing out before our very eyes. The intentional emphasis on our race, our sex, our this, our that, is the absolute intentional behavior of the political elite to pit us against each other and to distract us from the absolute usurpation of power taking place.

The fascinating thing about Joe Biden is that he is undeniably a part of the elite political system, but because he is (arguably) senile, he is unable to conceal his own condescending sentiments toward working-class and especially black Americans. He oozes condescension and superiority, and his diminished state of mind makes him unable to hide that from the masses.

ENDNOTES

[1] Brandt, Polumbo, Sanchez. "President Trump's Ban on Critical Race Theory, Explained." Foundation for Economic Education. September 14, 2020. https://fee.org/articles/president-trump-s-ban-on-critical-race-theory-explained/

[2] U.S. Bureau of Labor Statistics. "Characteristics of minimum wage workers, 2018," Report 1078, March 2019. www.bls.gov/opub/reports/minimum-wage/2018/pdf/home.pdf

[3] Marx, Karl, et al. The Communist Manifesto. Penguin, 2002.

[4] Ibid.

[5] Valley News Editorial Board. "Close The Gaps: Disparities That Threaten America." Bernie Sanders Website, October 2020. https://www.senate.sanders.gov/newsroom/must-read/close-the-gaps-disparities-that-threaten- America.

[6] The Anti-Defamation League. "Tattered Robes: The State of The Ku Klux Klan in the United States." https://www.adl.org/education/resources/reports/state-of-the-kkk

[7] United States Census Bureau. U.S. and World Population Clock. December 16, 2020. https://www.census.gov/popclock/

[8] Kryson, Moberg. "Trends in Racial Attitudes." Principles of Equality chart. Institute of Government and Public Affaris. https://igpa.uillinois.edu/programs/racial-attitudes

9   History.com Editors. "Tulsa Race Massacre." HISTORY. Updated June 23, 2020. https://www.history.com/topics/roaring-twenties/tulsa-race-massacre

10 Haskins. "Three Simple Rules Poor Teens Should Follow to Join the Middle Class." Brookings Institute. March 13, 2013. https://www.brookings.edu/opinions/three-simple-rules-poor-teens-should-follow-to-join-the-middle-class/

11 Centers for Disease Control and Prevention. "Preventing Child Sexual Abuse." https://www.cdc.gov/violenceprevention/childabuseandneglect/childsexualabuse.html

ACKNOWLEDGMENTS

In high school, I lost a constitutional essay scholarship competition. One of the directors of the program emailed me afterward, "Grace demonstrated during deep disappointment is an endearing quality." In other words, congrats on not crying until you got to your car.

Today, this work exists because he continued believing in me all the way through college.

Immeasurable thanks to that same man, Dr. John Baker, who gave me this chance to show me two things. First, there are men who can be trusted. Second, your life is remembered by the works you did for others with no expectation of return.

To my mother, Elizabeth Lee; my stepfather, Marvin Lee; my father, David Moore; and my grandmother, Glenda Huntley, thank you all for your incredible support during this project. I promise to never talk about socialism again...at least not during dinner.

Thaddaeus, Huntley, and Seth, thanks for being the best brothers.

To Jeffrey Thompson, Shreeya Singh, Mo Happy, and countless others who helped me in this endeavor, thank you.

To Dr. Antonio Saravia, for teaching the class that inspired this book, thank you.

ABOUT THE AUTHOR

Photo by Jadera Kraus

Madison Moore was the recipient of Joe Biden's infamous insult—"lying dog-faced pony soldier"—in February of 2020, during a college trip to the New Hampshire primary. She recently graduated from Mercer University with degrees in Economics and International Affairs. After contributing for the Libertarian organization Young Voices, she hopes to pursue a career in political writing and research.